Katharina Küsters
Handbook of Assistance Dog Training

AF155388

Handbook
of Assistance Dog Training

Part 1: Basics and Basic Commands

Katharina Kuesters

Impressum

Bibliografische Information der Deutschen Nationalbibliothek: Die Deutsche Nationalbibliothek verzeichnet diese Publikation in der Deutschen Nationalbibliografie; detaillierte bibliografische Daten sind im Internet über http://dnb.dnb.de abrufbar.

Die automatisierte Analyse des Werkes, um daraus Informationen insbesondere über Muster, Trends und Korrelationen gemäß §44b UrhG („Text und Data Mining") zu gewinnen, ist untersagt.

Verlag: BoD · Books on Demand GmbH, In de Tarpen 42, 22848 Norderstedt

Druck: Libri Plureos GmbH, Friedensallee 273, 22763 Hamburg

ISBN: 9783759768957

Contents

A Few Fundamental Words...3

Chapter 1: Basic Commands...24

    1.1 Out / No...24

    1.2 Heel...27

    1.3 Taking Treats Gently..31

    1.4 Walking Behind the Human..33

    1.5 Run or Go..37

    1.6 Left or Right Around...38

    1.7 Eat Slowly / Eat on Command..39

    1.8 No...42

    1.10 Place (Conditioned relaxation)...47

    1.11 Side Change..52

    1.12 Sit...55

    1.14 Taboo...60

    1.16 Wait...62

    1.17 Recall...63

    1.18 Back Up..67

Chapter 2: Basic Commands for Specialized Assistance Tasks.......................70

    2.1 Clicker Training...71

    2.2 Target Training..73

    2.3 Free Shaping...76

    2.4 Retrieving...79

    2.5 Go to... Person, Object, or Place..83

    2.6 Hepp..88

    2.7 Hopp..90

    2.8 Learning Names..91

2.10 Nose Touch..95

2.11 Distinguishing..97

2.12 (Crosswise) Standing...98

2.13 Paw Touch..99

Chapter 3: Tools..102

3.1 Collar...104

3.2 Harness..107

3.3 Leash...109

3.4 Dummy / Treat Bag..114

3.5 Additional Tools...115

    3.5.1 Clicker..115

    3.5.2 Target Stick...116

    3.5.3 Head Halter / Gentle Leader.....................................117

    3.5.4 Dog Backpack or Carrying Bags................................117

    3.5.5 Identification Vest...118

    3.5.6 Wheelchair Leash...119

    3.5.7 Autism Leash and Autism Harness.............................119

3.6 Behavior Interrupters..120

3.7 Animal Welfare Violation "Tools"......................................121

Preface to the Third Edition

What I had hoped for but did not expect has happened: my Handbook of Assistance Dog Training Part 1 is going into its second edition.

I am somewhat proud that so many people have incorporated my work into their daily training routines. I have received numerous feedback. Some of the suggestions I have been able to incorporate into this third edition. Some of the feedback was so individual that, unfortunately, I could not consider it.

What also brings me joy is that simultaneously with this second edition, the handbook will also be published in English. Numerous inquiries from English-speaking regions have motivated me to take this step.

I now wish you much pleasure and many inspirations while reading the new edition of the **"Handbook of Assistance Dog Tasks, Part 1: Basics and Basic Commands"**.

Sincerely, Katharina Küsters

Preface to the First Edition

For a long time, I have been fascinated by dogs that support people, replace a missing sense for them, or guide them safely through daily life and traffic. The training of an assistance dog takes a long time, a very long time. American trainers have calculated that fully trained assistance dogs (wheelchair companions or assistance dogs for veterans with trauma) have completed an average of 6,000 training hours. These training hours include not only the specific assistance tasks but also everyday things like housebreaking, acclimatization to environmental stimuli, unusual places and situations, and basic commands. Many people wish for an assistance dog by their side but do not have the financial means to afford such comprehensive training. This handbook is intended for these people and all other interested parties. Many times, clients and interested individuals have asked me for a foundational work. A handbook in which the most important basic commands are described and that can support self-training to become an assistance dog team.

Here it is, the Handbook of Assistance Dog Tasks Volume 1.

I wish you much joy and success on the path to becoming an assistance dog team!

Sincerely, Katharina Küsters

A FEW FUNDAMENTAL WORDS

Let's get one thing straight: The training of an assistance dog begins with a fundamental understanding of how dogs learn, how the principle of reward works, and which training tools are effective and when. An assistance dog must also learn the most basic commands such as sit, lie down, and wait. These basic commands not only make daily life easier and are often tested in many assistance dog team exams, but they also form the foundation for more advanced tasks and specialized assistance skills.

The training of an assistance dog, like any dog training, involves more than just responding to specific commands. For an assistance dog to work long-term, stay healthy, and perform joyfully, its needs must be met. Additionally, the handler must have knowledge of canine communication, the dog's needs, and how a dog learns. In short, they need a basic understanding of canine psychology.

Before delving deeply into the training of the assistance dog, I would like to address a few fundamental aspects regarding how dogs communicate and which commands make sense from a canine perspective.

Dogs primarily communicate with each other through body language, positions, and presence, often referred to as "energy." For a calm canine life within a pack, whether that pack consists of humans or dogs, adherence to four commands — or better termed, four rules — is sufficient:

1. Come here or stay with the group! In human language: recall and heel.

2. Give it up! In human language: drop it, fetch, off-limits, and also "no."

3. Stop that! In human language: stop and no. These two commands are often used interchangeably.

4. Be calm! In human language: settle and wait, take a break / place.

Additionally, it is beneficial to remember: a dog initially perceives its world primarily through smell from birth, followed by the opening of the eyes and, later, the ears. Being mindful of this in everyday life and training facilitates harmonious cohabitation with any dog. If a dog, for example, favors sight over scent, it may impulsively react to visual stimuli: chasing cars or wildlife, pursuing wild birds, or halting running children by nipping, are potential consequences. Conversely, a dog solely focused on sniffing may forget about its human through intense scenting.

Addressing these points comprehensively would exceed the scope of this manual. Therefore, I refer to our seminar offerings and books by my colleagues in "conventional" dog training with a focus on canine psychology.

I have received criticism after the first two editions for frequently recommending assistance from a (assistance) dog trainer when encountering potential difficulties. Yes, this is true, and I will continue this approach in this book as well. Some challenges can be overcome with a thought-provoking book or video. Some challenging behaviors may be resolved with an outside perspective from an experienced dog person. However, some behaviors of the dog may potentially harm itself, its human, or its environment. To intervene directly in such situations, preventing a situation or behavior from escalating, I strongly recommend involving an experienced (assistance) dog trainer from the very beginning of basic training.

Notice

_____

_____

_____

_____

_____

_____

_____

_____

_____

_____

_____

_____

_____

_____

_____

_____

_____

_____

_____

_____

_____

_____

_____

_____

_____

_____

_____

_____

Assistance Dogs and Commands

Beyond these four canine commands / rules, assistance dogs, in particular, learn many tasks that enable them to help their human or even save lives. Many of these assistance tasks stem from the four "canine commands." Assistance dogs enjoy working with their human, want to do something to make them happy, and emotionally thrive when praised. Assistance dogs are specially selected dogs that possess these qualities, among others: enjoy working, enjoy doing things together with humans, grow emotionally through praise, and visibly appreciate praise without becoming overexcited. With a dog exhibiting these traits, patient and positively reinforced training, loving consistency, ample patience, and an understanding of how the dog learns, thinks, and behaves naturally, assistance dogs can accomplish remarkable feats joyfully.

How does the dog learn?

Many dog experts and numerous textbooks delve into this question. Therefore, this manual will not detail how dogs specifically learn. Addressing this important topic would exceed the scope of this "Assistance Performance Handbook."

Important for the training of the assistance dog is:

The suitable dog, whether a puppy, adolescent, or adult, is trained lovingly, consistently, with much patience, considering individual reward possibilities, at their individual pace and according to their abilities and future requirements.

A stressed dog cannot learn. A dog that is afraid cannot learn either. Hunger, under-stimulation, or lack of physical exercise can also negatively affect a dog's behavior, making it unable to concentrate. With the right pace, suitable training methods, and good motivation, especially assistance dogs can accomplish astonishing feats. For a well-trained and eager-to-work assistance dog, twenty-five or even thirty commands are not a problem. Such a well-trained assistance dog also enjoys working for many years.

What can motivate a dog to work with and for its Human?

Assistance dog training is primarily based on the principle of positive reinforcement through treats / food or toys.

Reinforcements / Rewards

In this book, reinforcement and reward are used interchangeably. It always means something the dog wants more or prefers to do in that moment compared to what it currently has or is doing. A reward must always be of higher value. Herein lies a problem: the human must recognize what the dog wants in that moment or what motivates it and must know the dog well enough to offer a higher-value alternative.

An Example

The dog would rather greet its dog friend than neutrally walk past it with its human. One option is to maintain a distance from the other dog so that the own dog can focus on its human, and if the own dog calmly walks past with its human, both dogs can be released off-leash / with a long line on command.

Another Example

The dog carries around a shoe. If this is not its task at the moment, the human can call the dog over and exchange the shoe for a treat. But CAUTION: some dogs, after a few repetitions, carry around anything and everything so that their human calls them over and they receive a treat. In this case, please train the dog to pick up something only on command.

A second problem may arise if the dog quickly changes its motivation object. While the food pouch was the best reward last time, the next time it could be interacting with another dog. Therefore, it is important to observe and weigh precisely during training what motivates the dog in different situations and act accordingly.

A third common problem is dogs that are not very interested in food. Yes, there are picky eaters for whom food is not a motivator but a necessity to survive. These dogs are often hardly motivated by treats. With these dogs, the human often has to patiently discover what motivates them. Many of these dogs can be motivated with a short play session or even a small cuddle.

And then there are the very special dogs that cannot be motivated by food, stroking, or toys. With these dogs, an experienced trainer must carefully weigh whether they are truly suitable for the job as an assistance dog. A special characteristic of a good assistance dog is their ease of motivation and that they visibly grow with the praise of the human, appearing proud of having done something well.

VERY IMPORTANT:

The tips, hints, and instructions in this book have been checked and noted to the best of my knowledge and belief. However, an assistance dog is also a living being with an individual character and sometimes very unique ideas. In case of questions or problems, an experienced assistance dog trainer should be consulted immediately. In case of health complaints or problems, the advice of a veterinarian should be sought immediately.

Liability, regardless of direction, by the author is explicitly excluded. The implementation of the exercises mentioned here is at the risk of the dog owner.

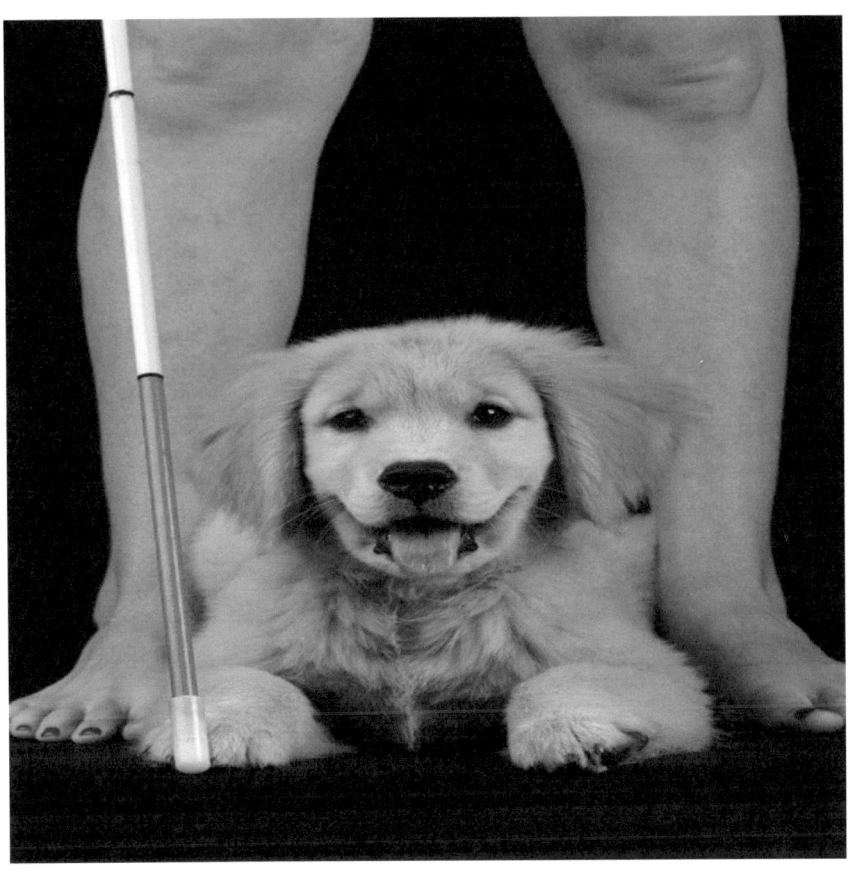

Rewards : What, When, How Much

A challenging topic that often sparks debate: rewarding dogs. Advocates ("YOU don't work for free either!") meet opponents ("For the dog, being able to do something for me is reward enough"). Whether there is one truth is difficult to ascertain. If so, it probably lies somewhere in the middle of these very contrasting opinions.

Before delving into the topic of rewarding the dog, let's explore some theory for better understanding. Originally, reward meant the "payment of wages" or "compensation, recognition, or honor" (Wikipedia, as of April 2019). In psychology, the term "reward" is now also used to describe a "reinforcer" (Wikipedia, as of June 2019). Against this backdrop, the theory emerges: "My dog shouldn't work for nothing, of course, he gets something for his effort." For many people, who also receive financial/material compensation (= reward) for their work (= effort), this is the only understandable approach.

In practice, there are people who naturally give their dog a reward (dog biscuit / treat) for every minor task accomplished, and those who only reward exceptional achievements (e.g., immediate recall) and plenty of variations in between.

A Look at the Two Extremes

The "always-for-everything-rewarder" and the "reward-only-for-special-achievements" person.

The "always-for-everything-rewarder" always carries treats and rewards every minor task, naturally and immediately (3-second rule). It's almost irrelevant whether the dog has accomplished a major task (e.g., coming when called from playing with its favorite dog buddy to the human) or something seemingly simple like a "sit".

A common problem is that many dogs, usually in adolescence, carefully weigh whether the reward from the human is better than what they are currently doing or have (want). Suddenly, the previously favorite treat is rejected because playing with the other dog seems more enticing. Next time, a "better" treat is brought out: sausage, cheese, or fish. But even this, from the dog's perspective, eventually loses its appeal to interrupt a nice game. What comes next? The Black Angus steak? The $100 fish? Eventually, it becomes difficult to always offer a "better" treat.

Another problem is that dogs also like to try to outsmart their humans. Following the motto "Show me the reward first, then I'll decide if it's worth it," many dogs wait until the human shows the reward. In practice, this may look like this: the human asks the dog to lie down. Previously, the "lie down" command was always followed with a treat in hand: the dog sits, the human's hand with the treat is slowly brought down in front of the dog's nose, the dog follows with its nose and lies down. So far, the theory. In practice, the treat is eventually omitted, and the dog remains sitting even though the hand is slowly moving towards the ground. Even though everything seems the same as before.

Many people then lack the patience to wait until the dog has finished thinking and lies down. They reach into the treat bag, the dog probably hasn't understood yet what it should do. This might even be true if the "lie down" exercise is still quite new. Perhaps the dog is also initially considering whether lying down is worth it. In most cases, the dog is correct: if the human is not fast enough, they reach into the treat bag, and the dog learns: "Aha, if the human says something and I don't react immediately, I get a reward (= treat), and then another one when I lie down."

The other type of person is the "reward-only-for-very-special-achievements" person.

Often, these dog owners also started as "always-for-everything-rewarders". The further the dog progresses in its training, the more confidently the commands are obeyed, the less frequently they are rewarded with something edible. Immediate recall and dog encounters are usually rewarded.

For many people, these are the two most difficult points, requiring a lot of training and therefore naturally possessing high value. Somehow understandable because apparently nothing motivates more than an occasional reward. If one never knows when a reward will be given, one will repeatedly exhibit a behavior in the hope that THIS time is the right moment. A problem may arise if unwanted behaviors are accidentally rewarded. For example, someone who has problems with dog encounters and tries to distract their dog with a treat from another dog (showing it at the beginning of the situation and possibly letting the dog "try" it), may reward at the wrong moment and thereby reinforce the unwanted behavior.

In the context of the three-second rule, this can lead to the dog learning: "If I sound the alarm early that another dog is approaching, I get a reward, and if I get even more worked up while passing the other dog, I get even more." This is the (possible) thinking of the dog. The human probably had the idea: "Oh, he's stressed because there's another dog coming, I'll distract him with a treat, and if he's quiet for one or two seconds, he gets a reward immediately, then at three seconds of calmness..." Two completely different assessments of the same situation.

What Makes a Good Reward?

The best reward is always what the dog currently desires or something better. This is not always easy. If the dog wants to interact with another dog, but for some reason, that dog does not want closer contact, it becomes difficult. An alternative could be to offer the dog interaction with the human, to play with them.

But how does the human find out what they can reward their dog with? A collection of ideas has proven useful here:

1. What is a nice reward for simple exercises? (the usual food, for example)

2. What is a slightly higher-value reward for more challenging exercises? (waiting amidst distractions)

3. What is the perfect reward when things get difficult? Interruption of a game, for example.

4. What is the absolute top-tier reward for truly challenging situations?

Of course, this collection of ideas is not perfect from day one; it evolves during the first few weeks together and should be critically reviewed and supplemented regularly. It is also important: The super-hyper-mega-treat / game is really only given in absolute exceptional situations such as encounters with wildlife or similar. Also, rewards lose their effectiveness if they are used too often. In assistance dog training, much is done with motivation through treats / food. Especially in specialized training, that is, the training of specific assistance tasks, good treats help. However, the dog must be able to reliably perform the basics and basic commands without regular rewards up to this training step.

But another point is also important when it comes to rewards: Timing, i.e., the right moment.

Notice

The Three-Second Rule

Modern learning psychology posits that a reward must be given within three seconds to be effective. Any longer, and the rewardee (the dog) forgets why they're being rewarded, potentially linking the reward to a different action. This three-second reward rule poses a significant challenge for many people. Some individuals need a lot of practice WITHOUT the dog to master the timing of the reward so that the dog is appropriately rewarded for its behavior.

Others may not be able to reward quickly due to a disability or illness. In such cases, it's essential to consider who else can reward the dog or what other alternatives exist. One possibility is having an experienced dog trainer teach the dog the "clicker" principle and then "click" during training, allowing the handler to reward the dog at their own pace.

Another alternative is to replace the clicker with a sound that's easier to produce. Many people with motor issues in their hands use tongue clicking as a signal that the dog has performed well.

Intermediate Bridge

Anyone involved in dog training will eventually come across this term. The intermediate bridge is a training method that uses an "anchor" or "anchor word." The dog is trained to understand a word or whistle that means: "Hold on a bit longer; you're on the right track!" This concept is similar to the children's game "Hot and Cold," where one person, blindfolded, searches for a pot by hitting it with a wooden spoon while others guide them with "warm" (right direction) or "cold" (wrong direction).

The intermediate bridge works similarly. It theoretically replaces the word "warm," signaling to the dog, "You're on the right path" ... to the reward. This technique is especially popular for recalls, reinforcing that the dog is on the right track during a double recall.

The ideal sequence is: The handler addresses the dog—the dog turns towards the handler—the handler calls the dog back—the dog comes and is reinforced by the intermediate bridge until reaching the handler.

For puppies, sometimes during puberty, or when recall is still being established, the intermediate bridge proves useful. Its effectiveness for a trained, adult dog is subject to individual judgment.

According to common understanding, the dog shouldn't stray so far from the handler that such support is necessary.

Some handlers use the intermediate bridge for other exercises: heeling, tracking, or tricks involving held positions, such as lying on the side.

How long should a dog train?

This is a challenging question without a universal answer. Younger dogs have shorter attention spans compared to older dogs. Some dogs need more time between exercises to process what they've learned. Additionally, with assistance dogs, training isn't limited to basic commands and skills; socialization also plays a significant role.

A useful guideline is the formula: One minute per week of the dog's age per day, with no more than one minute per month of the dog's age in a single session, followed by sufficient breaks. Thus, a twelve-week-old puppy can train for a total of twelve minutes a day, but no more than about three minutes at a time on specific commands.

If the dog is too excited, overly active, or struggles to settle down, the training was likely too intense, too long, or too demanding. In such cases, it's advisable to slow the pace and schedule more rest periods.

This formula has its limits. For most dogs, three fifteen-minute sessions of intense, focused training a day are generally sufficient.

CHAPTER 1: BASIC COMMANDS

The purpose of basic commands is to reliably guide the dog in various situations. Basic commands are standard in the assistance dog tests of major organizations. Some of the basic commands are trained and tested both on and off-leash. What exactly belongs to the testing standards of the chosen organization should be requested from them.

The training of basic commands begins with every dog training, whether it's an assistance dog, therapy dog, protection dog, or rescue dog. Only good basic obedience, which includes basic commands, ensures the acceptance of assistance dogs and thus the access and accompaniment possibilities of the trained assistance dog. Basic commands are usually not difficult tasks. However, they require great care in execution, training, and, of course, a lot of patience.

In this book, I limit myself to the basic commands that, in my experience, are most frequently used in everyday life or are mentioned in the examination requirements of the current Assistance Dog Ordinance.

1.1 Out / No

An interruption signal is required in the AHundV as a "training content for all forms of assistance dogs." Often, "Out" and "No" are used for the same task: The dog should spit out what it has in its mouth. The difficulty often is that people become too hectic and try to take away from the dog what does not belong in its mouth. However, dogs often reluctantly give up their "prey": Either because they have not learned to, because they do not take their humans seriously, or because, from their perspective, it is not worth it.

Assistance dogs usually learn from an early age not to pick up anything unauthorized from the ground and to give everything back. This requires a lot of patience and training, and it is often a real challenge to keep the dog's nose or mouth off the ground.

Goal: On the word and/or hand signal "Out" / "No," the dog spits out EVERYTHING and ANYTIME whatever it currently has in its mouth.

Required Equipment: Clicker and a really good reward, possibly collar/harness with a leash to secure the dog, toy, large chew items, socks… everything the dog likes to take in its mouth but is large enough not to be swallowed immediately. Safety is, of course, self-evident.

For **advanced learners:** Meat sausage sandwiches, liver sausage, fish… things that dog haters often lace with poison or shards and lay out as bait.

Training Setup

In the first step, the dog learns that it is worthwhile to spit things out because there is something even better in return. First, the dog is allowed to work on a large chew snack, a toy, or something similar. After a few seconds, the human distracts the dog's attention by luring and shows the dog the particularly good treat in hand. If the dog lets go of, for example, the chew snack, the sock, or whatever it had to reach for the treat in hand, it receives the command "Out" or "No" and is rewarded with the treat from the hand. Those with really good timing can click the dog at the moment of letting go and then have a few more seconds for the reward.

CAUTION: Until the dog reliably follows the command "Out" / "No," only use SAFE training objects! Only when the dog always and immediately spits out, for example, an ox tail, dried tripe, or smelly socks, should you start with smaller or more difficult objects.

CAUTION: Never, but really never, run after the dog during this exercise. Running after teaches the dog only to swallow forbidden things faster so the human cannot get to them. The same applies to putting your hand in the dog's mouth: This is also absolutely taboo! The dog learns only how quickly it has to swallow so the human has no chance.

It is better to start with sufficiently large things and, if necessary, prevent the dog from running away with a collar/harness and leash.

If there is concern that the dog may have swallowed something unhealthy/poisonous or otherwise dangerous, consult a vet and, if necessary, go to the animal clinic.

The **hand signal** for "Out" / "No" is three fingers quickly and energetically moving downwards. The index and middle fingers are extended, the thumb is attached to the index finger.

1.2 Heel

The command "Heel," in the form of a relaxed accompaniment of the dog with and without a leash, is also part of the general training content for all assistance dogs. Many people think that "Heel" and "walking on a loose leash" are the same. In terms of the AHundV, this can be interpreted that way. However, the correct "Heel" command means that the dog walks with its shoulder at knee height of the human and continuously looks at the human, either on a loose leash or off-leash. This position is very uncomfortable for the dog and is usually not needed by an assistance dog. However, "walking on a loose leash" means that the dog walks relaxed next to the human and adjusts to the human's pace. It does not matter whether the dog is on a leash or not.

This description is about "relaxed walking next to the human" without overtaking, with a loose leash or off-leash. An apparent contradiction: "A dog learns to walk on a loose leash only with a loose leash." What sounds contradictory is explained by physics: When the dog pulls, it experiences resistance at the other end of the leash and a feeling of tightness on its neck or chest. It gets used to it and will continue to pull. Only when the dog learns to feel a loose leash (no counter-pull from the human and no tightness on the neck or chest) and is rewarded for this feeling will it experience walking on a loose leash as something pleasant.

Goal: On the command "Heel," the dog walks relaxed at a consistent distance in the position specified by the human, without pulling on the leash, without corrections by the human, and over a longer distance.

Required Equipment: A short leash (1 meter is usually enough), well-fitting collar or harness, reward, possibly clicker.

For advanced learners: "Wheelchair leash," "Autism leash," possibly "short lead."

Training Setup

It is important to start training the leash walking directly upon the dog's arrival and always be consistent. It confuses the dog if it is allowed to pull sometimes and then not again. Initially, it is often advisable to lead the dog in training for the "leash walking" exercise with a well-fitting collar and, in free time, when it can walk on a slightly tense leash, with a harness. Dogs usually learn this distinction quickly. It is only important that the dog should not pull so hard on the harness that it endangers itself, its human, or others.

When walking on a loose leash, it does not matter whether the dog walks on the left or right. What is important is that it adjusts its pace to the human and does not switch from one side to the other without command.

A medical alert dog may run a little ahead. Some alert dogs cannot fulfill their task if they (supposedly correctly) walk next to or even behind the human. However, medical alert dogs do not pull on the leash. They run a little ahead of the human, but the leash is loose.

For all other dogs, the rule is: If the dog walks in the desired position, it is calmly praised. At the beginning, many dogs walk only three or four steps on a loose leash on one side. This is normal and will be extended in the course of training.

If the dog walks in a different direction or pulls, the human stops and ignores the dog. As soon as the dog realizes it cannot continue, it will reorient itself to the human. This is the right moment to address the dog. If it walks to its human, the human continues calmly until the dog pulls again. After a short time, the dog will turn to the human more quickly when the leash tightens. Now, the human stops as soon as the leash tightens and insists that the dog comes back to its side.

Some dogs pull especially at the beginning of the walk. Consider whether the dog might urgently need to relieve itself, has too much pent-up energy, or if you may have set off in an excited mood.

For particularly persistent leash pullers, switch walks or orientation walks may help. These should be shown and explained by an experienced trainer to avoid accidents. Sometimes, it is just a small thing in the behavior or body language of the human that causes the dog to persistently pull on the leash. An outside perspective can work wonders.

For people with little hand strength or coordination difficulties, there are various aids for training. Head halters, different leashes, and harnesses should, however, always be temporary aids until calm walking with and without a leash is securely trained. Not all commercially available aids are recommended or approved for use. Therefore, I strongly advise consulting an experienced dog trainer if there are difficulties.

If the human is unable to influence their (pulling) dog at all or is to be connected to the assistance dog, for example, with a "wheelchair leash," the leash training MUST work reliably. A pulling dog connected to its handler with a wheelchair leash or jogging belt endangers both its human, itself, and its surroundings.

I repeat this point gladly once again: In these cases, leash walking must be reliably mastered before the dog walks for the first time with its handler and a leash.

Also, please remember: All kinds of head halters, leashes, and harnesses are ultimately aids that should not be used permanently. The goal is always not to need these aids permanently. Special aids for assistance dogs, such as autism leashes, support harnesses, and the like, are naturally excluded from this!

The **hand signal** for the command "Heel" is the extended index finger of the hand pointing downward on the side where the dog is to walk.

1.3 Taking Treats Gently

Many people have experienced that dogs do not take treats gently from the hand, but instead, the whole hand ends up in the dog's mouth. This can be unpleasant and, for children or people with sensitive skin, not entirely safe. Even if the dog doesn't mean any harm, bruises from these canine "snapping turtles" are quite possible.

Goal: On the command or hand signal for "Gently," the dog takes the offered treat GENTLY from the hand.

Required Equipment: Clicker, small food rewards of different qualities, possibly (garden) gloves.

Training Setup

Ideally, the puppy learns from the beginning that haste and greed won't get it anywhere. A treat is taken in hand, using a (garden) glove for particularly greedy dogs, and the hand is closed into a loose fist. Now, hold the closed fist towards the puppy/dog. The dog will likely try to get the treat by nibbling, nudging, or scratching. If the dog is gentle, keeps its mouth closed, and uses more of its nose, the fist slowly opens, and the dog may take the treat. If the dog starts to use its teeth or paws to get the treat faster, the fist closes quickly and without comment.

Repeat the process. Most dogs learn very quickly, often within 5 to 10 repetitions, that they get the desired treat faster if they are gentle. If the dog looks at you in between: GREAT! The hand opens, and the dog can take the treat immediately.

If the dog loses interest, open the fist a bit, move it closer to the dog's nose, and encourage the dog to try again. Usually, these gentle dogs don't need to train the "taking food gently" exercise for long and intensely. Once your dog has learned to take an offered treat gently from your hand, you can expand this exercise, for example, with a treat on the knee. Here, a treat is placed on the leg, covered with a hand, and the hand only lifts when the dog is gentle.

Once this works well, introduce other people so that the dog learns to be gentle with EVERYONE. At this point, future assistance dogs also start training the command: Take food only after being prompted by another person.

1.4 Walking Behind the Human

In some situations, it is necessary for the dog to walk behind the human. The dog walks relaxed directly behind the person, without dawdling or sniffing, and without sticking its head past the person's leg to see what's ahead.

Goal: On the command or hand signal for "Walk behind," the dog aligns itself behind the person and walks relaxed and promptly behind them.

Required Equipment: Clicker, treats, ideally a food tube, possibly a target-stick, and initially a wall or a narrow passage made of fence elements.

Training Setup

If the dog has learned to follow the target stick, this can be used as a magnet behind the person's back. It is important to keep the right height so the dog doesn't try to reach the target stick by jumping or is tempted to sniff the ground.

If the dog is not familiar with the target stick or the person doesn't want to use this tool, proceed as follows: Take a few treats in one hand and hold this hand behind your back. Depending on the size of the dog, flexibility may be required. For very small dogs, the treat hand often has to be brought through the legs to the back, so the person walks with a hunched back in a "waddle walk." For large dogs, it is usually enough to hold the treat hand relaxed on the lower back. Then, the person starts walking. The dog should stay with its nose at the hand/food tube and thus walk behind the person.

In the next step, the food is left out, but the hand continues to act as a "magnet" behind the back. Now, the command "Behind" is introduced and reinforced.

In the third step, the passage of fence elements or at least a one-sided barrier (wall, house wall, fence...) is used. The hand is now only briefly brought behind the back at the beginning and as needed. The dog should walk behind the person on the command "Behind." Now, the clicker can also be used for reinforcement. The dog is fed, of course, where it performs the exercise: Behind the person's back. If the dog tries to get ahead in this third step, its way is blocked, and the hand is again used as a magnet. Many repetitions and consistent execution help the dog understand the command.

The **hand signal** for the command "Behind" is either a head nod back-wards or a fist with the thumb extended backwards.

1.5 Run or Go

The "Run or Go" command marks the end of an exercise. A trained assistance dog knows that with the command "Run," all previous commands are lifted, and it has free time.

Goal: The word or hand signal for "Run" signals to the dog that a task is finished and no further commands will follow for the time being. The dog has "free time."

Required Equipment: Clicker, small rewards.

Training Setup

From the very beginning, every command is ended with a "Run." It is important to catch the exact moment BEFORE the dog breaks the command on its own. For most dogs, at the beginning of training, these are a few seconds that the dog remains in the command. For example, the process is quite clear with "Sit": The dog is brought into the "Sit" position and should stay there until another command follows. At some point, faster or slower, the dog will get up from sitting, scratch itself, or lie down. It is crucial to catch the moment before the dog does this.

When the dog sits, after a few seconds, say the word "Run" and simultaneously give the hand signal for it. Whether the dog stands up, lies down, or stays sitting after the "Run" command is its decision. The dog has free time at this moment. Gradually, the duration of the sitting is extended. It is important that the dog rarely breaks the command on its own (e.g., stands up), but the person ends the exercise. When clicker training, it is important: The click occurs where the dog performs the exercise. At the beginning, it is sensible to reward the dog there (in the position or situation). When sitting, this means in the "Sit" position and BEFORE the dog stands up.

Later in training, the click occurs in the desired situation, and the reward comes later. The advantage of this method is: The dog does not break the command or situation on its own to get its reward.

The **hand signal** for the "Run" command is a sweeping hand movement beside the human body, as if the person were pulling a tablecloth off a table behind them.

1.6 Left or Right Around

In many situations, it is useful to send the dog around a large object. Sometimes the path is blocked by a trash can, a small wall, or something similar.

Goal: The dog should, on command, move away from its person and go around an obstacle in the way. It should not sniff the ground, the roadside, or other people, not mark, and promptly return to the person's side.

Required Equipment: Clicker, treats, possibly a target stick, larger objects that can block the path like trash cans, pylons, low fences....

Training Setup

First, it is important that the dog walks relaxed beside its person without a leash. It should not dawdle or run ahead, not sniff the ground, or lift its leg. The person walks with the dog towards the obstacle. The person walks so close to the obstacle that the dog cannot squeeze through. Now, the hand on the side where the dog walks is used as a magnet (possibly with a treat in the hand) and guided to the "other" side of the obstacle. Ideally, the dog follows the hand and is immediately praised. After a few repetitions, most dogs follow the person's hand even without a treat. Now, the person says the command "left" when the dog should pass the obstacle on the left or "right" when it should pass on the right.

CAUTION: Even when the dog is moving towards the person, directions are named from the DOG'S perspective! Only then does the dog correctly pass with the object on its left side (command "right") or on its right side (command "left"). Many dogs find it helpful if the corresponding hand is extended for support. But be careful: If the dog follows the hand and this is inevitably pulled back, the dogs often come back too! They follow the hand as they have learned. Therefore, it is better to lead the hand in a "sending" motion or extended over the obstacle.

The **hand signal** for "Left" or "Right" around is the extended arm on the corresponding side, which is moved in a flowing motion with the palm forward from back to front.

1.7 Eat Slowly / Eat on Command

Dogs are gulpers. There may be a few picky exceptions, but normally, dogs devour their food in large chunks and very quickly. Nowadays, this is usually unnecessary for household dogs: The bowl is refilled regularly, often several times a day. There are, of course, various aids like anti-gulping bowls or other things that are supposed to make the dog eat slower. However, this section describes another method that makes many dogs eat more slowly. The prerequisite is that the dog does not show aggression around food or resources and has a normal, healthy nutritional status. If the dog shows any aggression related to food or other resources, seek advice and support from an experienced trainer!

Goal: The word and/or hand signal for "slow eating" also includes patiently waiting until the bowl is on the ground and the food is "released" for the dog to eat. Only then is the dog allowed to start eating.

Required tools: Food in multiple portions, food bowl, and if necessary, a collar/harness and leash to secure the dog.

Training Setup:

This exercise is actually one of the simplest, but it requires a lot of time and patience. Regardless of what the dog does, the handler must never become impatient, angry, disappointed, or frustrated. These are all emotions that the dog cannot understand or might misunderstand in connection with food. If necessary, the dog is secured with a collar/harness and leash, held by a second person, or alternatively secured to a stable hook.

Now, fill the food bowl with a small initial portion of food. The dog does not receive a command at this point. The dog is expected to be calm and wait on its own. If the dog is loud or very restless, the activity is paused and only resumed when the dog is calm. If the dog remains calm, it is slowly fed by hand. If the dog stays calm during this, the bowl is placed on the ground and secured with a hand or foot. If the dog remains calm, the bowl is slowly and calmly pushed towards the dog, and the dog is allowed to eat. During this time, the dog is left undisturbed.

Once the small portion is eaten, the whole process is repeated: lift the bowl, fill it with a portion, and so on. It is important that the dog is neither completely starving nor very excited during this exercise. After many repetitions, the dog learns that it only gets to eat when it is calm. It also learns that it doesn't need to gulp down everything at once.

Once the dog understands this, the second step is introduced: the dog is only allowed to eat upon command. Again, the bowl is filled and the dog must wait until the handler "releases" the bowl. To do this, the bowl is shielded with a hand or foot, and only when the dog is truly calm is it "released." In a further step, the dog learns to take something edible only with permission from another person.

The **hand signal** for "slow eating" is a welcoming gesture with the hand.

1.8 No

Just like the reliable recall and the command "Stop," the small word "No" can save lives: for example, when a dog wants to eat something unhealthy or even dangerous, or wants to go somewhere where there are dangers. However, it is one of the commands that many people find the hardest. Often, there is a fear of rejection behind it. People often worry that their counterpart will no longer "like" them if they say no to something. However, dogs seem to think differently in this regard and take a "No," meaning a prohibition, calmly. Furthermore, the command "No" also serves as an interrupter. Upon hearing the command, the dog learns to stop what it is doing and turn to its person. The person must follow the command "No" with a second command so that the dog knows what it should do instead.

Goal: At the word and/or hand signal for "No," the dog stops what it was about to do and redirects its attention. A "No" always requires a second command that tells the dog what it is allowed or supposed to do instead.

Required Equipment: Clicker, reward, something the dog likes, such as a toy.

For advanced: Many different stimuli that the dog likes and the appropriate rewards.

Training Setup

Place a treat or toy on the ground and cover it with a hand or foot. Lift the hand or foot slightly to spark the dog's interest. If the dog's nose or paw approaches the treat/toy, cover it again and say a firm "No." If the dog moves away even a little, turns its head, lowers its paw, or looks at the person, it gets a reward.

Problem: For many people, the words "No" and "Fine" sound similar. However, one word means a prohibition, while the other means praise or reinforcement. Many people, therefore, use the English word "No" for "Nein." An energetic "No" is understood by many dogs as what it is: a prohibition.

Advanced training: Practice "No" in different situations but always in a way that you can control the situation.

The **hand signal** for "No": The raised index finger moving back and forth in front of the dog's face.

How it shouldn't be: In use, the assistance dog should not sniff objects unless it is part of its tasks.

1.9 Down

A reliable "down" command is listed in the Assistance Dogs Ordinance as a "training content for the basic training of all types of assistance dogs." In practice, a reliable down, often combined with waiting, has proven effective. The "down" command means that the dog immediately lies down, regardless of the surface, the distance between the dog and the person, and distractions in the environment.

Goal: At the word and/or hand signal for "down," the dog lies down reliably, regardless of the surface, distance to the person, distractions, or what the dog was doing before.

Required Equipment: Clicker, reward, different situations & surfaces, e.g., blanket, cushion, carpet,... later also elevated surfaces.

Training Setup

Dogs naturally lie down when they are tired or very relaxed. Some dogs also lie down to get a treat that is under something. There are three different ways a dog can lie down:

A relaxed lie down, where the hind legs are often on one side and the front legs are stretched out or bent.

A so-called "working down," where the front legs are stretched forward and the hind legs are parallel on both sides of the body. In the working down position, the dog looks ready to spring, awaiting further commands.

Lying on the side, usually in deep relaxation or sleep. For the "down" command, the so-called working down is needed. The relaxed down with both hind legs on one side is needed for other exercises (Exercise 1.10 "Place"). For puppies, both spontaneous lying down (working down) and the "down" command are reinforced. For targeted training, the dog is attentive and focused on the person. The person holds a small treat between the thumb and middle finger and lowers the hand with the palm facing down in front of the dog's nose to the ground. The treat stays in place. The puppy will follow the hand with its nose until it ideally lies down. Some dogs will lower their front body but keep their rear end up. In this case, patience is needed until the rear end also goes down. As soon as the dog is fully down, the command "down" is given, and the puppy gets its reward.

After a few repetitions WITH the treat, it is left out, and the dog lies down expectantly at the "down" command. Now it's time to reinforce the "down" with the clicker and then reward with a treat. In the next training step, the distance between the person and the dog is increased, and also the time the dog has to stay down before getting its reward. The dog also learns to lie down on different surfaces from the beginning. After many repetitions with good reward timing, the dog will quickly understand that "down" means to lie down. Some dogs have great difficulty lying down completely. Some lack coordination, and some lack trust. In these cases, the dog can be guided carefully by a bent knee. If the dog still does not lie down voluntarily, a medical cause could be behind it. This should be clarified by a vet. If there is no medical cause, an experienced dog trainer can help.

Hand signal for "down": The open hand, with the palm facing down, is lowered in front of the body towards the ground.

Lay Down

1.10 Place (Conditioned relaxation)

The "place" command is a relatively new command. It involves the dog associating a defined spot (place) or a tool (the "marker" sign) with relaxation. This exercise initially requires a lot of patience and countless repetitions. Once the dog has internalized the command, it can relax quickly even in unfamiliar situations. This is especially difficult at the beginning for alert dogs, signal dogs for hearing impairments, and dogs living with people who have high inner tension. Since these dogs are always on alert, they must first learn to relax without completely neglecting their task and person.

Goal: The word and/or hand signal for "place" signals the dog to a trained (conditioned) relaxation in all situations.

Required Equipment: A "marker" sign such as a dog leash, a small cloth, a blanket, clicker, and treats.

Training Setup

For the first steps, it is crucial whether the dog is older and already knows the word "down," or if it is a puppy being trained. With a puppy, training "place" begins immediately after moving in. The puppy is given a marker, such as a small blanket, a guest towel, or similar, in its sleeping basket when it is tired. Place it near the head so the puppy can see the marker. When the puppy wakes up, the marker is removed until the next nap. As the puppy gets older, the marker is also taken to other places, and the puppy is placed on it entirely or partially. The marker should never be associated with action, excitement, or play. It is solely for training conditioned relaxation. If the dog is already older and knows how to lie down relaxed, it is brought to or moved onto the marker by free shaping (explained further). Many dogs find it difficult to relax in unfamiliar environments or during long train or car rides. Here too, the "place" command can help induce conditioned relaxation.

IMPORTANT: In its "place," the dog has its peace. This is especially important for children who often need to learn to give a dog rest periods. If the assistance dog's tasks include cuddling sessions with the person, these are not conducted in the "place"!

Also **IMPORTANT:** If the assistance dog feels that its person needs support or if the alert dog warns its person, it will always leave the command. This is called "intelligent disobedience."

Hand signal for "place": There is no hand signal. The marker, whatever it may look like, is the signal.

Notice

1.11 Side Change

Almost all assistance dogs should learn to walk on both sides of their handler. An exception is guide dogs for the blind, who typically stay on one side. It's important for these dogs to change sides behind the handler on the command "side change." If the dog crosses in front of the handler, accidents are likely. Another exception is assistance dogs whose special leash is attached to a wheelchair, for example. These dogs switch sides in front of the handler to avoid leash tangles and potential accidents.

Goal: On the word or hand signal for "side change," the dog switches behind the handler from the left to the right side or vice versa. An exception is dogs wearing a support harness; they switch sides in front of their handler.

Required Equipment: Clicker, treats, possibly a target stick.

Training Setup

Initially, the dog (with or without a leash) is guided on one side. The handler takes several treats in both hands and stands still. In this example, the dog is on the handler's left side. The handler then slowly moves their LEFT hand backward to the spine level. The RIGHT hand joins and takes over the dog's snout, which ideally has followed the hand up to this point. The right hand then slowly moves forward again. If the handler performs this step slowly enough and the dog is attentive, the dog should now be on the right side with its snout at the right hand.

The dog receives a treat from the right hand and walks a few steps on the right side. Then the right hand moves backward to the spine level, where it meets the left hand, which now takes over the snout and slowly guides it forward. The dog gets a reward on the left side and walks a few steps on the left side of the handler. When these changes work while the handler is standing, the command for each side ("Left" or "Right") can be introduced.

In the next step, the handler walks slowly while the treat-filled hands guide the dog like a magnet. Once this works well, the treats are gradually phased out, and the dog receives praise (or a click followed by a treat) when it arrives on the named side.

The **hand signal** for the side change is a hand indicating the desired path of the dog. To switch the dog from left to right, the left hand swings behind the back.

1.12 Sit

A reliable sit command is also a fundamental part of the basic training for all types of assistance dogs and is mentioned in the AHundV. On the command "Sit," the dog should sit down immediately and everywhere without first approaching the handler.

Goal: On the word or hand signal for "Sit," the dog reliably sits down regardless of the surface, distance from the handler, distractions, or what the dog was previously doing.

Required Equipment: Clicker (if the dog is familiar with it), treats, various surfaces during training (including elevated ones like a small platform or a step), and different distractions (traffic, other people, other dogs/animals...).

Training Setup

Although dogs naturally sit, the "Sit" command needs to be trained. For puppies, both spontaneous sitting is reinforced and the command "Sit" is deliberately trained. For targeted training, the dog is attentive and focused on the handler. The handler places a small treat between their thumb and middle finger, extending the index finger straight up. The treat remains in place. This hand slowly moves up in front of the dog's nose, prompting the dog to sit down to keep the treat in view. As the dog's rear moves towards the ground, the command "Sit" is given, and the dog receives the treat.

After a few repetitions with the treat, it is removed, and the dog sits on the command "Sit" expectantly. It's then time to reinforce the "Sit" with the clicker and reward with a treat. The time between the click and the treat is initially so short that the dog does not break the sit to get the reward. In the next training step, the distance between the handler and the dog is increased, and the duration the dog must sit before receiving the reward is also extended. Additionally, the dog learns from the start to sit on various surfaces (carpet, tiles, grating, grass, mats, steps, platforms...). After many repetitions with good reward timing, the dog will quickly understand that "Sit" means to sit down.

The **hand signal** for "Sit" is an upward-pointing index finger, moved from bottom to top in front of the body. Alternatively, an open hand with the palm facing up.

Sit Down

1.13 Stop

It is still unclear whether a stop signal is classified as an interruption signal according to AHundV. However, it is certainly sensible to be able to stop the dog from a distance. Stopping from a distance is an important command and can sometimes save a dog's life. This might sound exaggerated, but anyone who has seen a car appear on a path and almost hit a running dog will understand the importance of this command.

There are two ways to stop the dog: one where the dog is running ahead of the handler and is stopped from behind, and another where the dog is stopped while approaching the handler (frontal view). Both variants are equally important and are discussed here.

Goal: On the command "Stop," the dog immediately halts and, if necessary, assumes a predefined position.

Required Equipment: Clicker, reward, possibly a toy, a well-fitting harness, and a ten-meter long line.

Training Setup

Stopping when the dog is running towards the handler:

The dog must reliably return! The dog is placed on a blanket/mat. The handler slowly walks backward, creating a distance of about five to ten meters. The distance depends on the dog: smaller or slower dogs around ten meters, faster dogs about five meters. The dog waits in the designated spot. The handler stands at the chosen distance and watches the dog. The handler holds a toy the dog likes in their stronger hand.

The handler calls the dog and simultaneously raises the hand with the toy up or forward (depending on what is easier for the dog). When the dog takes two to three steps, the hand snaps forward to the highest point, but the toy does NOT fly; it stays in the hand! It is crucial that the movement stops at the highest point! The dog will stop to see where the toy goes. This moment is rewarded! After that, the toy can be thrown a short distance as a reward.

Some dogs look at the handler's waist height rather than up. For these dogs, the toy is "thrown" from below. It is advisable to practice this motion without the dog first. After a few repetitions, the dog will stop at the arm movement. Now, the "Stop" command is introduced. It must be spoken very energetically, as it is a lifesaving command and should be pronounced accordingly. If the dog can already sit or lie down at a distance, the "Sit" or "Down" command follows after the stop word.

IMPORTANT: Only one out of ten recalls should include a stop. Otherwise, the dog might hesitate to return happily and might wait first.

The reward is given where the dog stopped! For the stop command, this applies to both the "Click" and the reward itself.

Stopping from behind the dog:

This variant is a bit more complicated and should be trained only when the dog already knows the "Stop" command from the frontal view and is physically mature. In this version, the long line is attached to a well-fitting chest harness. Depending on the dog's size or weight, the handler either holds the long line (for lighter dogs) or attaches it to a very sturdy hook/post. The dog sits beside the handler, who has a toy in hand. The toy is placed on the ground at a short distance (about seven to eight meters with a ten-meter long line). The dog waits in a sit position. The handler releases the dog to get the toy after making eye contact. Quick reaction is needed! The "Stop" command must be given before the line tightens. Ideally, if the dog knows the command from the first exercise, it will stop and look confused. Then, the "Sit" or "Down" command is given and executed immediately. The dog is rewarded on the spot.

If the dog does not stop immediately, the distance should be reduced, and the "Stop when recalling" exercise should be continued.

IMPORTANT: The chest harness must fit perfectly, and the long line and hook/post must be in excellent condition. The toy should be placed at a slightly shorter distance than the long line's length to avoid sudden braking. Holding the long line by hand is recommended only for very light dogs and well-trained handlers. Beware of accidents!

The **hand signal** for "Stop" when the dog is approaching the handler is a hand moving quickly over the head and stopping at the highest point.

There is no **hand signal** for stopping the dog from behind or while the handler is walking.

1.14 Taboo

"Taboo" is a command signaling to the dog that something is "forbidden." This could be objects the handler is holding, such as toys, laundry, or a baby, as well as items like a toy or dummy the handler has taken from the dog. It can also refer to the handler's body, which the dog should not jump on.

Goal: On the verbal and/or hand signal for "Taboo," the dog either gives the handler space (if the handler's body is taboo) or refrains from touching an object (toy, dummy, clothing, etc.).

Required Equipment: A toy, food dummy, or another item the dog desires.

Training Setup

First, show the dog the toy (or desired object). Once the dog shows interest, hold the item close to your body and keep it still. If the dog tries to jump to reach the object, quickly move your hand up and down in front of your body while saying "Taboo." If the dog accidentally gets touched on the nose or head by your hand, it's not a big issue and usually isn't harmful. It simply means the dog was too close to you. Continue the movement until the dog gives you space. If the dog moves away from the object, such as by sitting a short distance away while showing interest, praise the dog and make it clear that this behavior is desired. After a few repetitions, the dog should start responding to the "Taboo" command by maintaining distance and giving the handler space.

The **hand signal** for "Taboo" is a flat hand, palm facing the body, moving quickly up and down close to the handler's body.

1.15 Forward

Just like the command "Back," an assistance dog should also learn "Forward," which means moving ahead of the handler on command. This is particularly useful for tasks such as fetching help, checking rooms or corners, and approaching a person (e.g., an autistic child).

Goal: On the verbal and/or hand signal for "Forward," the dog moves in a straight line in the indicated direction until given a new command.

Required Equipment: Clicker, treats, and optionally, a small mat, carpet square, or sticky note if the dog is familiar with these.

Training Setup

The easiest way to teach this is by training the dog to go to a mat, small carpet square, or sticky note and touch it (see "Go to" and "Paw Touch" in Chapter 2). Once the dog has learned to go to a designated spot, place it at a short distance in a straight line. Send the dog to this touch point. As the dog moves towards it, click and reward at varying distances. Alternatively, without a mat, show the dog an outstretched hand pointing straight ahead and reward any step the dog takes in the indicated direction. "Forward" can also be trained through shaping.

The **hand signal** for "Forward" is an outstretched arm pointing in the desired direction.

1.16 Wait

"Wait" means the dog pauses until given an alternative command. This command is often combined with another command: sitting and waiting, holding something and waiting, etc. The AHundV mentions "Wait" in combination with sitting and lying down as part of basic training for all assistance dog types.

Goal: On the verbal and/or hand signal "Wait," the dog waits calmly and patiently until given another command, such as "Take it."

Required Equipment: Clicker, treats, and depending on the task, a food bowl, retrieve object, etc.

Training Setup

Waiting is a challenging task for many dogs, especially puppies who often struggle to hold back and wait, such as waiting for the handler to pass through a door first. An exception applies to dogs trained to check rooms or block exits. Begin training as soon as the dog arrives. For instance, always pause at every door and wait until the dog sits or stands calmly. Only then, allow the dog to go through the door on command. This practice extends to waiting at street corners, curbs, traffic lights, crossings, stairs, etc., based on future assistance tasks.

If the dog pauses on its own at a door, curb, traffic light, etc., introduce the command "Wait." Gradually increase the duration the dog must hold a position by adding seconds over time. For example, progress from "pick up the retrieve object" to "pick up and hold" until given a new command.

The **hand signal** for "Wait" is an open hand held in front of the body with the palm facing forward.

1.17 Recall

A reliable recall is essential for off-leash freedom. Only an (assistance) dog that can be recalled in any situation can enjoy this freedom and move away from its handler—always within the range where recall is dependable. According to AHundV, recall is also part of the basic obedience training.

Goal: On the verbal and/or hand signal for "Recall," the dog returns to its handler immediately in any situation. There are two types of recall:

1. Simple Recall: The dog comes back without needing to take a specific position near the handler.

2. Precise Recall: The dog takes a predefined position, such as sitting on the handler's left side, after returning.

Required Equipment: A well-fitting harness, a long leash (five to ten meters), treats, and possibly a clicker.

Training Setup

Simple Recall (Come)

For a simple recall, it's enough if the dog stops what it's doing and runs back to the handler. It doesn't matter if the dog sits, stands, or even does a headstand by the handler. It's also irrelevant whether the dog comes to the left or right side or sits in front of the handler. The most common command for a simple recall is "Come." In practice, "Come" can be problematic because it's used frequently in various contexts and can confuse the dog. Better alternatives include the English "in," the French "ici," or the commonly used English "come on." It's crucial to always use the same word and associate it exclusively with positive experiences: In the first months, the dog should always receive a reward at the end of a simple recall. Those training with a whistle can use a short double whistle.

Training for the simple recall begins from day one, whether the dog is a puppy or an adult. The handler calls the dog by its name once, immediately followed by the recall command (e.g., "come on"). Once the dog reaches the handler, it is immediately rewarded.

Initially, the dog should already be moving toward the handler or focusing on the handler when called. During the first weeks, the dog may not understand the command, so it needs to learn the meaning of the "sound sequence." Soon, the dog will understand that a great reward awaits it by the handler if it quickly responds to the recall command.

At the start, having a few treats in a pocket or a food dummy can attract the dog's attention. As the dog runs toward the handler, the simple recall command is given. When the dog reaches the handler, the handler takes a few steps back, giving the dog a few small treats as a reward. The dog will follow the handler, who moves backward and rewards the dog for doing so.

Once this works well in a low-distraction environment, increase the distractions and the distance between the dog and the handler. For a juvenile or adult dog, a long leash might be necessary to support the training. The long leash prevents the dog from moving out of the handler's influence range and ignoring the recall. At the same time, it allows the dog a small radius of "freedom."

Handling a long leash requires practice and is best demonstrated by an experienced trainer in a personal session. While a long leash can be a great tool, incorrect use can pose dangers to the handler, the dog, and the environment.

Precise Recall

In a precise recall, the dog takes a well-defined, trained position at the end. Usually, this is a "sit" in front of the handler at arm's length. Some handlers prefer the dog to sit or stand by their side. Each end position has its pros and cons. For instance, if the dog sits in front of the handler, the handler has to lean forward to leash the dog, which some dogs might perceive as threatening, causing them to back away. Handlers with limited mobility might find it difficult to lean forward to leash the dog.

Some handlers first call their dog to sit in front and then call it to their side. This is possible but requires two commands, which can often be combined into one. If the dog sits or stands by the handler's side, it must learn not to get in the handler's way or bump into them.

The training for both positions is the same: In the first step, the handler uses a treat or toy to guide the dog into the desired position. Click – command (e.g., "here") – click, and the dog gets its reward. In the second step, the dog should move into the desired position by itself when called, still receiving a lot of support and with minimal distractions.

In the third step, the dog orients itself towards the handler, runs over a short distance, and takes the desired position, still with some support and low distractions.

In the next step, both the distractions and the distance are increased.

In the final step, the dog moves freely, responds quickly and happily to the recall command, and takes the trained position. Once this works in every situation, from any distance, and in various environments, the precise recall can be used in challenging situations.

The **hand signal** for the precise recall is an arm raised vertically in the air on the side where the dog should come.

1.18 Back Up

"Back Up" is a crucial command for situations where the dog is in the way and there isn't enough room to pass by. This command is also helpful when working with a wheelchair or walker to move the dog out of the way. Many dogs initially struggle to walk backward, especially in a straight line. This requires a lot of practice and patience.

Goal: On the "Back Up" command, the dog steps backward. The dog should walk as straight as possible to avoid health issues.

Required Equipment: Clicker, treats, possibly a target stick, and if available, sturdy child gates, a stable wooden fence, or a wall.

Training Setup

Many dogs have no idea what to do with their hind legs when they start training to walk backward. Therefore, it's crucial to build this exercise very slowly and step by step. Ideally, the dog is already fully grown and healthy. Young dogs can learn to take a few steps backward, but only a few steps to prevent health problems. If available, use sturdy child gates to create a narrow passageway, wide enough for the handler and dog to move through together but narrow enough to prevent the dog from turning around.

The handler leads the dog into the passageway, stops before reaching the open end, with the dog behind them. Then, the handler turns around and slowly walks toward the dog without applying pressure. Ideally, the dog will take a step back. This first step is immediately rewarded!

If the dog sits or lies down, it should be brought back to a standing position. A sitting or lying dog cannot back up. If the dog jumps up at the handler or tries to turn around, the pressure applied by the handler was too high. In such cases, the pressure must be immediately reduced. It's also important not to look directly into the dog's eyes (which can be seen as threatening), but rather to gaze softly over the dog at the point where the dog should back up. Later, open one side of the passage, so the dog is only confined on one side. Advanced handlers guide their dog backward without any side constraints in any situation.

Since the handler can appear quite threatening while walking toward the dog, this exercise requires a lot of sensitivity and a good understanding of the dog. If in doubt, this exercise should be demonstrated and supervised by an experienced trainer.

The **hand signal** for "Back Up" is a flat hand held at hip height, signaling the dog to move back.

Notice

_____

_____

_____

_____

_____

_____

_____

_____

_____

_____

CHAPTER 2: BASIC COMMANDS FOR SPECIALIZED ASSISTANCE TASKS

In the first chapter, this book covered basic commands that are standard in most assistance dog exams. This chapter will focus on foundational commands that do not fall under basic obedience but are essential building blocks for specific assistance tasks.

For example, the assistance task "Bring the phone when it rings" requires the dog to master several foundational skills: the dog must retrieve objects (not just a food or training dummy), run to a named object (the phone) on command, respond to the phone ringing (either on its own or on command), bring the phone to its handler, and hold it until the handler takes it.

Almost all assistance tasks can be broken down into individual components in this manner. Ultimately, assistance tasks are composite commands that make life easier or even save lives.

Over time, several commands have emerged that are repeatedly used in various assistance tasks. These include the commands "Retrieve," "Touch" (with nose and/or paw), "Go to," "Pull," "Stand at a designated position," and "Hold."

Additionally, there are three training methods that, while not commands themselves, significantly facilitate the cooperation between handler and dog: clicker training, target training, and "free shaping." These three methods will be described first.

2.1 Clicker Training

A clicker is a tool that allows precise reinforcement of a dog's behavior. Most clickers consist of a small box with a metal strip inside that makes a "click" sound. The dog learns that each "click" promises a reward, usually a treat, but sometimes a toy. Using a clicker requires some practice, and the dog must first be conditioned to the clicker.

It's best to learn how to use a clicker from an experienced trainer and practice without the dog at first, perhaps with a human partner. Only when the handler's timing is right should the dog be "clicked." Poor timing can quickly lead the dog to learn incorrect associations and unwanted behaviors.

Required Equipment: Clicker, food rewards

Goal: Condition the dog to the clicker, meaning the dog associates the "click" sound with a forthcoming reward.

Training Setup

Once the handler understands and internalizes the principles of clicker training, the dog is conditioned to the clicker. In the first step, a treat is offered immediately and simultaneously with the click sound. For dogs that are not highly food-motivated, the handler must find a suitable reward.

After several repetitions, the treat is given two to three seconds after the click. Ideally, the dog looks expectantly at the handler or at least at the hand that previously delivered the treat when it hears the click.

In the third step, the treat is given only after the dog looks expectantly at the handler following the click.

It's important that the dog does not leave its position upon hearing the click to get closer to the hand. The reward is always given at the point where the exercise or task was successfully executed. If the dog leaves its position, it is brought back to the correct position without any verbal cue and only then rewarded. In the fourth step, the dog is clicked for completing a task or a partial step of a task and then rewarded in that situation.

2.2 Target Training

A target is a tool that provides the dog with a clear indication of where to touch an object or person. The word "target" comes from English and means "goal." The entire hand or a single finger can theoretically be a target.

A target stick is a small box, often combined with a clicker. Inside this box is an extendable stick, usually about 60 cm long, with a colored ball at the tip. In training, the handler holds the combined target clicker in one hand, simplifying coordination.A target is a tool that provides the dog with a clear indication of where to touch an object or person. The word "target" comes from English and means "goal." The entire hand or a single finger can theoretically be a target.

A target stick is a small box, often combined with a clicker. Inside this box is an extendable stick, usually about 60 cm long, with a colored ball at the tip. In training, the handler holds the combined target clicker in one hand, simplifying coordination.

The target is held with the tip (the small colored ball) where the dog is supposed to touch something with its nose. Once the dog understands the concept of the target, it can be trained from a small distance or at a point that is difficult for the handler to reach.

Goal: The dog touches the (colored) tip of the target with its nose, learning to touch objects, items, or people with its nose.

Required Equipment: Clicker or target clicker, food rewards

Required Basic Skills: Clicker training

Training Setup

If the dog is not familiar with the clicker, it is first conditioned to it. Once the dog understands the principles of clicker training, target training can begin. Initially, any interest the dog shows in the target stick is reinforced (clicked). After a few repetitions, only interest in the (colored) target tip is reinforced. After a few more repetitions, only touching the (colored) target tip is reinforced. If the dog touches the box in the hand, the middle of the target stick, or uses its teeth or paws, there is no reinforcement—no click. The target stick is held loosely in the handler's hand in a position easily accessible to the dog. It is important that the dog's nose moves to the target, not the target to the dog's nose.

Once the dog understands that it gets a reward when its nose touches the (colored) target tip, the position of the target can be gradually changed. In further conditioning, the target is moved to increasingly difficult positions for the dog: very close to the ground, elevated in the air so the dog has to support itself to reach the (colored) target tip, under the handler's leg, and so on. Once the dog consistently touches the target in various positions, the target can be used in training. The handler must always be fair and give the dog a realistic chance to safely reach the (colored) target tip.

2.3 Free Shaping

The term "free shaping" comes from English, like many terms in dog training, and means "free shaping" or "free form." In free shaping, the dog is gradually guided through many small steps to achieve a larger or more complex task. The dog offers its own solutions for how to accomplish a task. Successful clicker training is essential for accurately rewarding the dog's behavior.

Many dogs need to learn the concept of free shaping. Older dogs that have been trained through commands may need to relearn how to think for themselves.

Goal: In free shaping, the dog works out a task on its own and learns to act independently. This is especially important for assistance dogs that need to act without human instruction in emergencies (e.g., guiding to safety, pressing an emergency button, interrupting panic attacks).

Required Equipment: Clicker, food rewards, possibly a small box, paper, or an object to be conditioned.

Required Basic Skills: Clicker training

Training Setup

If the dog is not yet accustomed to working independently, a small box filled with crumpled paper and treats can be used. The dog is encouraged to engage with the box, and any interaction (even small ones) is rewarded with a click and a treat. As training progresses, the steps become larger, and the expectations increase.

If the dog is already familiar with independent work, free shaping can begin directly. A desired task, such as touching a colored sticky note with its nose or paw (Touch), is broken down into the smallest possible units. Each small unit or action in the right direction is rewarded. For the "Touch" exercise, decide whether the dog should touch with its nose or paw, as both have advantages and disadvantages and may be useful in different situations. Some dogs also have a preference for touching with their nose or paw.

In the first step, a brightly colored sticky note is attached to the handler's hand or leg. If the dog touches the note with its paw or nose (depending on the desired action), click and reward.

In the second step, the dog should touch the note for a few seconds or multiple times in succession, depending on the desired task. Click and reward after a longer touch or multiple touches.

In the third step, the attentive dog is encouraged by the handler's gaze or finger point to touch a colored note placed a short distance away. When the dog touches the note, say "Touch," click, and reward simultaneously.

In the final step of basic conditioning for the "Touch" command, the attentive dog is sent to the colored note with the command.

Next, it's time to train the dog to go to different locations or objects, as described in the "Go to..." command. Once the dog understands "Touch" and "Go to... (object)" including distinguishing different objects, it can learn to touch various items on command. If the dog hesitates, break down the "Touch" exercise into smaller units: looking at the note, stepping towards the note, walking to the note, touching it, etc..

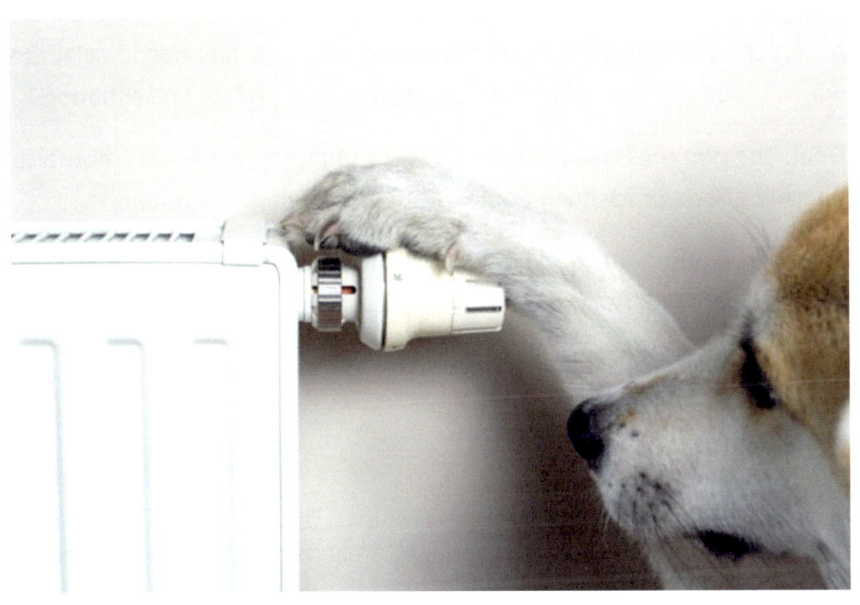

2.4 Retrieving

Retrieving involves the dog bringing a named object to its handler on command. The command can be a word, a hand signal, or a learned situation. It is also essential that the dog understands a reward system (such as clicker training) and enjoys it. The dog must carry the object to the handler or a defined point and hold it until given another command. Dropping the object on the way does not count as a retrieve.

A dog can reliably retrieve on command only if it has been socialized with various surfaces, objects to carry (including metal), and situations.

Goal: The dog runs to a named object, carefully carries it in its mouth to its handler or a predefined point without damaging or dropping it.

Required Equipment: Clicker, food rewards, a food dummy, or the object tobe retrieved.

Required Basic Skills: Clicker training

Training Setup

Depending on the dog's type, initial interest in the object to be retrieved is encouraged (free shaping), or directly rewarding the dog for carrying the object.

Many dogs enjoy retrieving a food pouch/dummy. It's important that the food dummy can be closed with both Velcro and a zipper. Most dogs can easily open a Velcro closure to access the food.

The purpose of the food dummy is to teach the dog that it only gets the coveted food if it brings the pouch to its handler, who then opens it. Note: Bringing prey, especially edible prey, to another is entirely illogical from the dog's perspective. Prey is not shared among "predators" (which includes dogs). The dog must have great trust in the handler to willingly "give up" its prey.

At the beginning of this exercise, it might be easier for many dogs to wear a well-fitting harness and be secured with a long leash (five or ten meters). In the first step, fill the food dummy in front of the dog's nose, and allow the dog to take one or two pieces directly from the pouch. CAUTION: Some dogs are very eager and may dive directly into the pouch. In this case, first practice the command "take food gently."

Now close the food dummy and hold it out to the dog. If the dog shows interest: click and give a small reward directly from the dummy.

In the third step, place the food dummy a few steps (maximum half the leash length) away and send the dog to it. Hold the leash! When the dog reaches the dummy, wait and observe. Catch the moment when the dog has the dummy in its mouth but has not started chewing on it. At that moment, move in the opposite direction and shorten the leash. It's important to keep walking, encouraging the dog to follow. As long as the dog carries the dummy, continue shortening the leash until the dog is next to the handler.

When the dog is next to the handler with the dummy in its mouth, the handler turns calmly and holds the leash slightly taut to prevent the dog from lying down, placing a hand under the dummy without touching it.

The slightly taut leash prevents the dog from lying down, and the hand under the dummy does not pose a threat or suggest "prey fighting." Eventually, the dog will drop the dummy. At that moment, click and reward the dog from the dummy.

If this third step works well, the handler remains stationary. The dog should now bring the laid-out dummy to the handler on its own to get the reward.

In the fifth step, gradually extend the time the dog holds the dummy. Ideally, the dog knows from clicker training that an exercise is not over until the click is heard.

In the sixth step, the leash is gradually let go and eventually omitted.

The dog should now retrieve the food dummy on command and hold it until the handler instructs it to release.

If the dog reliably retrieves the food dummy in various situations without a leash, other objects can be introduced into the training. For metal or very smooth objects, it may be helpful initially to wrap the object in a grippy piece of cloth, making it easier for the dog to pick up. As training progresses, the cloth can be gradually removed until the dog retrieves even metal or very smooth objects.

Some dogs, particularly retrievers, naturally retrieve various objects from a young age. This behavior can be immediately incorporated into training: with appropriate reinforcement and praise, these dogs will have little trouble later retrieving keys, metal bowls, or coins.

However, be cautious: some dogs may develop an obsession with retrieving to get a reward, even without a command. An obsession often self-rewards, making it difficult to interrupt this unwanted behavior, which may require the help of an experienced trainer.

Especially with puppies and at the beginning of training, ensure the objects to be retrieved are safe and cannot be accidentally swallowed.

2.5 Go to... Person, Object, or Place

If the dog knows the command "Go to..." and has additionally learned to distinguish between people, places, or objects, many assistance tasks are possible.

Goal: On the command "Go to...", the dog moves towards the named object, place, or person, even overcoming obstacles or the resistance of its handler who might not be able to lead at that moment.

Required Tools: Clicker, treats, a helper person, the object or place the dog should go to.

Required Basic Exercises: Clicker, free shaping, distinguishing objects and people, nose touch.

Training Setup

Go to... another (helper) person

If the dog is supposed to go to another person on command, for example, to fetch human help, the dog first learns the name of the other person (Exercise: "Learning names"). Once the dog has internalized the name of the other person, both the handler and the other person stand about ten meters apart. Both people have treats in hand, and one of them additionally has the clicker (if used for training).

The dog starts with the handler. The second person lures (not calls) the dog while the handler simultaneously says "go to... (name of the helper)". When the dog reaches the second person, it gets a click and a reward from the second person (remember the command "take food from strangers!").

The handler then calls the dog back. This exercise is repeated several times, ensuring the dog only moves to the second person after the lure and the release from the handler.

This first step can be well combined with the command "Go to..." and "Sit from a distance" or "Wait".

When the dog moves towards the second (helper) person upon the lure sound, the handler can give the command "Go to..." as soon as the dog starts moving.

In further training, the distance between the people is increased, and difficulties such as different rooms, stairs, or doors that need to be pushed open are introduced.

In the end, the dog should reliably and directly run to the named person on the command "Go to... (name of the helper)", possibly overcoming obstacles.

Depending on what is desired, further assistance tasks can be derived from the command "Go to... (helper person)": the helper person can be motivated to follow through a predetermined sign (bring item), or do something alone upon the dog's arrival.

Important: For many years, assistance dogs were trained to run to strangers in an emergency and make them follow. This has proven impractical in practice. Many people are afraid when an unfamiliar dog runs towards them and may bark demandingly.

Additionally, the risk of accidents should not be underestimated. If the dog reliably wants to execute its command in an emergency, it will not pay attention to traffic or other dangers but will carry out its task (fetching help) as quickly as possible.

The hand signal for "Go to... (helper) person" is a sending away hand movement. Optionally, a special hand signal for the helper person can be included.

Go to... (Place)

Unlike a helper person who acts independently depending on the task/assistance needed, "Go to... (place)" should direct the dog to a named place. These are usually seating areas, exits, a building wall, or the front door.

The dog must also act against the resistance of its person and lead them to the named place in an emergency. This often occurs when the handler is unable to identify and head towards a "safe place" during a frightening situation.

Goal: On the command "Go to... (place)", the dog first learns to recognize the named place from a few centimeters away. Here, the example "Go to bench (= seating area)" is described for simplicity.

Required Equipment: Clicker, treats, various seating areas.

Required Basic Commands: Clicker, free shaping.

Training Setup

In the first step, the dog learns that a seating area is called "bench." It doesn't matter initially if the bench is an actual bench, a low wall, a chair, or a large, flat stone. The dog is led to one of these seating areas and encouraged to touch it with its nose or front paws. When the dog touches the bench, the clicker sounds and a reward is given.

Some dogs only recognize a bench when a treat is placed on it. In this case, a bench is stocked with treats, the dog is led there, and it may eat the treats. Each treat is associated with the command "bench" and individually clicked.

This exercise is practiced with different "benches." Initially, it is always trained from a short distance, recognizing and touching a bench. Once the dog has learned different "benches," the distance between the person and the bench is gradually increased. In the third step, the dog must spot a seating area on its own and go there. It is effective to include a short training session (with a vest) on each walk, where various commands are practiced.

The command "bench" can be practiced well in a park with many benches, low walls, or large flat stones. The dog is then motivated during the training session to independently show EVERY bench.

After the short training session and the command "Run, free time," the dog's indications are ignored unless the person is in an emergency situation.

Usually, there is no hand signal for "Go to... (place)." Of course, the handler can think of an individual hand signal and train it.

2.6 Hepp

With "Hepp," the dog jumps up with its front paws onto something while its back paws remain on the ground. "Hepp" can help, for example, to leash the dog from a wheelchair or to operate a light switch. The command "Hepp" should only be trained with an adult dog. As preparation, younger dogs can train to place their front paws on a low elevation (a step, for example).

Goal: On the command "Hepp," the dog places its front paws on the indicated spot and remains standing with its back paws on the ground. The dog stays relatively still during the command.

Required Equipment: Clicker, treats, possibly a pedestal, a step, or a chair.

Required Basic Exercise: Clicker.

Training Setup

The attentive dog is motivated to place its front paws on a slightly elevated surface. During training, the dog is encouraged to place its front paws higher and higher. Some dogs follow a treat in the human hand. Other dogs enjoy learning this command through free shaping.

The hand movement for the command "Hepp" is formed by the index and middle fingers of one hand tapping on the spot where the dog should place its front paws.

2.7 Hopp

"Hopp" is the command for the assistance dog to jump onto something or into a car. The assistance dog waits, before jumping into the car, until it receives the command "Hopp"; this is standard in most tests. Likewise, the assistance dog does not jump onto anything without the "Hopp" command, unless necessary to perform a task. Puppies are taught early on to only jump onto something with the "Hopp" command. Of course, the height and frequency are always adjusted to the dog's age! The younger the dog, the less frequent and lower the jumps should be.

Goal: On the word or hand signal for "Hopp," the dog jumps onto the indicated object, such as into a car or onto a bed.

Required Equipment: Clicker, treats, various elevated surfaces to jump onto.

Required Basic Exercises: Clicker, free shaping.

Training Setup

Whenever the person lifts the dog into the car, they say "Hopp car." When the dog is a bit older, it can learn to jump onto a low pedestal. Most dogs enjoy jumping onto an elevated spot, so the command "Hopp" is usually easy to train. More challenging is preventing the dog from jumping uncontrollably onto everything (bed, sofa, armchair, chair...). Here, consistency in everyday life is the only help. An older dog can be encouraged with a treat to jump onto something. The command "Hopp" can also be well trained through free shaping.

The **hand signal** for the command "Hopp" is the hand tapping on the spot where the dog should jump.

2.8 Learning Names

Dogs can learn to associate different people with specific names.

Goal: The dog learns to distinguish people by their names. In later training, the dog will learn to go to the named person on command, either because the handler has sent them or because the handler is unresponsive and the dog needs assistance.

Required Equipment: A helper, and later in the training, two or three helpers, a clicker, treats.

Required Skills: Clicker training, free shaping.

Training Setup

Although the underlying purpose of this exercise can be very serious, the training itself is quite entertaining. The handler selects at least one other person (later in training, multiple people) to participate, such as family members or coworkers. Ideally, at least one of these people will be the helper in later training. The handler and the other people stand facing each other (if there are two people) or in a circle. The initial distance should not be too great to prevent the dog from getting distracted by sniffing. Each person has some treats hidden from the dog's view. The dog starts in the middle of the circle or next to the handler.

Now, the other people take turns calling the dog using the word "Come" plus their name. It is crucial that only one person calls at a time to avoid confusing the dog. This helps the dog associate the person with the command "Come (plus name)." The dog is called alternately from one person to another ("Come (plus respective name)"), and when the dog reaches the person, it is rewarded. Once the dog has finished its treat, the next person calls, like in a ping-pong game.

If the dog goes to the wrong person, that person simply does not react. No reaction means no eye contact, no touching, no speaking, and ideally not even thinking about the dog. Without success at the wrong person, the dog will quickly turn to another person and will be rewarded when it reaches the correct one.

As the dog becomes better at distinguishing names, the distance between people is increased. Later, various rooms, stairs, doors, or small obstacles can be added to the training.

2.9 Pulling

The pulling exercise can be a real challenge for very submissive and insecure dogs. What a hand is to us, the mouth is to a dog. If a higher-ranking dog grabs prey, a submissive or insecure dog will immediately let go. In this case, the distance between the dog's mouth and the person's hand must be sufficiently large, perhaps using a long rope or a glove.

Dogs can use the pulling skill to open drawers and doors, remove clothing, pull an emergency bag from a shelf, or similar tasks. Do not start practicing "pull" until after the dog has finished teething. Puppy teeth are still very loose in the jaw and can be easily lost when pulling.

Goal: On the verbal and/or hand signal command "Pull," the dog takes the indicated or named object in its mouth and pulls until given another command.

Required Equipment: Clicker, food reward, play rope, old towel, or something similar for the dog to pull on.

Prerequisite Skills: Clicker training, free shaping.

Training Setup

The dog is motivated to play with a play rope, a toy rope, an old towel, or something similar. When the dog pulls on the "prey," the person initially pulls gently, later more strongly, while simultaneously giving the pull command.

In the second step, the pull rope is attached to the item the dog should pull, such as a door handle, or the towel is threaded through the sleeve of a jacket, pant leg, sock, glove, hat, etc. In the third step, generalization occurs, and the dog learns to pull the indicated or named object on command.

The **hand signal** for "Pull" is a closed fist moved from top to bottom.

2.10 Nose Touch

In the nose touch exercise, the dog touches a named object, a defined point, or, for example, a finger or the person's leg with its nose. The purpose is for the dog to operate a light switch, elevator button, or even an emergency call button when instructed by the person. Many dogs enjoy the "Touch" command and may start touching things with their noses without a command. It is therefore important that the "Touch" command is carefully trained and only rewarded upon command.

Goal: The dog learns to touch a defined point with its nose.

Required Tools: Clicker, food reward, blue or yellow sticky note, later a target stick.

Prerequisite Skills: Clicker training, possibly target stick, treats.

Training Setup

Some dogs naturally touch an outstretched finger or the tip of the target stick with their nose. This behavior is rewarded, and a verbal command is later added as the difficulty is gradually increased. In the first step, click as soon as the dog's nose touches the finger/target stick. In the second step, hold the finger/target stick a bit higher or to the side. When the dog touches the finger/target stick with its nose, click.

Only when the dog reliably touches the offered finger/target stick with its nose, without chewing on it or taking it in its mouth, is the verbal command introduced. Once the dog touches the finger/target stick reliably on command, the finger/target stick is held against the object the dog should touch, such as a light switch. The command is now "Touch light." When the dog reliably touches the light switch with the attached finger/target stick, the finger is gradually removed, and the dog should touch the light switch on command.

Some dogs have difficulty touching an offered finger with their nose. In this case, touching a small sticky note can be rewarded. Any interest in the colorful sticky note is rewarded, the position of the sticky note is slowly changed, and the difficulty is increased.

Eventually, the dog will no longer need the sticky note as a cue. Gradually, additional objects can be incorporated into the training and named accordingly.

A **hand signal** for the nose touch can be chosen individually by the handler.

2.11 Distinguishing

Distinguishing involves the dog learning to bring or touch only a named object or go to a named person.

Goal: The dog reliably goes only to the named object or person.

Required Equipment: Clicker, food rewards, and depending on the exercise, several familiar and unfamiliar objects or helpers.

Prerequisite Skills: Clicker training.

Training Setup

First, the dog is familiarized with an object, such as a key. This is most easily done using clicker training and then naming the key without any other objects nearby. If the dog reliably goes to the key when given the "Key" command, regardless of where it is placed, another, distinctly different object, like an old phone, is introduced into the training. The phone is also trained without the distraction of the key (using clicker training). When the dog reliably goes to the phone on the "Phone" command, regardless of where it is placed, the phone and key are placed some distance apart. The dog is then sent to one of the two objects, key or phone, and is only rewarded if it goes directly to the named object.

Once the dog can reliably distinguish between two objects, additional objects are trained using the same method and gradually combined with the other objects.

The process for distinguishing people follows the same principle. The only difference is that the named person gives the dog a reward, while the incorrect, unnamed people ignore the dog.

A **hand signal** for distinguishing is not provided.

2.12 (Crosswise) Standing

Crosswise standing is needed in various exercises, the two most common being "Support" and "Block."

Goal: The dog stands (crosswise) in front, beside, or behind the person on command and remains standing.

Required Equipment: Clicker, food rewards, possibly a (hand) target.

Prerequisite Skills: Clicker training, "Stand" command.

Training Setup

Lure the dog with your hand into the position crosswise in front of you. Once the dog is standing crosswise in front of you with all four paws on the ground, click and reward. Release the dog from the position and lure it back into the position. After several repetitions, you can introduce a command, click, "good stand," and treat. Initially, give the command "Stand" when luring the dog into position. After many repetitions, the dog should independently move into the crosswise position in front of or behind you on the "Stand" command. Practice the command with distractions, in various locations, and in different positions.

The **hand signal** for "crosswise stand" is an outstretched hand with the palm pointing where the dog's nose should go, or alternatively, a pointing finger.

2.13 Paw Touch

On the "Paw Touch" command, the dog should touch your hand, leg, or a named, defined point with its paw. By touching your hand or leg, the dog can alert you to something important. By touching an object with its paw, the dog can, for example, turn a floor lamp on or off.

Goal: Immediate and targeted touching of a hand, leg, or defined point with a paw.

Required Equipment: Clicker, food rewards, blue or yellow sticky notes.

Prerequisite Skills: Clicker training.

Training Setup

Just as you trained "Nose Touch" with your dog, now train "Paw Touch." The command "Paw" is recommended, as it clearly differs from "Touch" used for "Nose Touch." Clicker train the targeted yet gentle touch of your hand, leg, or a defined point and gradually increase the difficulty.

It's important to reward only gentle touches without the use of claws (unless a firm touch is explicitly desired). Reward the "Paw Touch" only if you have given the command or if the dog offers the paw touch in an emergency. Otherwise, there is a risk that the dog will use the "Paw Touch" as a begging gesture and employ it uncontrollably.

A **hand signal** for "Paw Touch" is not provided.

CHAPTER 3: TOOLS

A common question is: Why is the topic of "tools" discussed in a book about basic training? My answer is always the same: Because tools are an important topic. Dog training, whether for assistance dogs or family pets, rarely occurs without tools nowadays. At the same time, many different opinions exist regarding various tools, and some are completely pointless or hardly usable in assistance dog training.

Tools are widespread in dog ownership today. Often, their purpose is clear and quickly understood. Sometimes, their purpose seems incomprehensible, and some are even considered cruel by today's standards… and new tools are introduced almost weekly.

Ultimately, all tools are merely aids or objects that facilitate the coexistence of humans and dogs. Dogs do not use tools among themselves; they rely on their presence and communication skills.

The most important communication tool is something humans always carry with them and do not need to acquire: their presence and authority, their charisma, and their love for the dog. Due to legal regulations (such as leash laws or car safety requirements), some tools seem almost mandatory: a collar or harness, a leash, and a safety device in the car. All other tools are debatable. Here, only the various types of tools will be introduced, with their advantages and disadvantages highlighted.

In the training of assistance dogs, various tools are used to facilitate collaboration and the everyday life of the handler. These include, for example, a (guide dog) harness, a support harness for balance issues, a target stick, carry bags or dog backpacks, or a small retrieve object as a signal. There are also various specialized assistance dog leashes such as autism leashes, wheelchair leashes, etc.

The following will discuss various general tools and, of course, specialized assistance dog accessories.

NOTE: Some tools sold on the market are considered cruel and their use
is legally prohibited! These tools usually cause pain or fear and are therefore not allowed in dog training in Germany.

To help non-professionals recognize these tools, they will be described
at the end of the chapter.

3.1 Collar

Collars are placed around the dog's neck and fastened. They can have a leash attached, and they also provide a visible place for a dog license tag and a pet registry tag. Collars come in countless varieties, sizes, materials, and price ranges. They may feature decorations, plastic buckles, metal clasps, lack adjustment options, or have printed names, emergency numbers, or other information. The selection and design possibilities are nearly endless.

There is often much debate regarding the size of the collar. Some prefer very narrow collars, while others prefer very broad ones. Both sides have plenty of arguments for their favorite and against the other variant. Ultimately, the dog owner must decide what works best for them and their dog.

Quality should not be compromised when it comes to collars. Once a dog is fully grown, a good collar can often be worn for a lifetime. In an emergency, the collar can be a lifesaver! If a dog tries to chase a deer or run across the street to another dog, the collar must fit properly, withstand significant force, and be escape-proof.

The main types of collars are:

a) Fixed-size Collars made of leather, webbing, or Biothane, with or without decorative trim. These can be adjusted to the neck size using a slider or multiple holes.

b) Slip Collars with Stop: These are usually round-stitched, made of leather or webbing, sometimes Biothane or braided. Slip collars are set to a maximum tightness with a small stopper. Thus, the collar is loose in regular use and tightens under tension (e.g., in danger). This tightening is limited to prevent choking. Slip collars are often safer for dogs that slip out of regular collars (which is very common). Additionally, slip collars are easy to put on and take off, making them suitable for people with limited hand or arm strength. Once adjusted to the maximum size (open), the dog can learn to put the collar on by itself.

c) **Hunting Collars:** Frequently seen in hunting dog shops, these are simply another term for standard collars. Those who do not hunt their dogs will not need specialized collars like "tracking collars" (worn when searching for injured game) or signal collars (wide rubber collars with reflectors).

d) **Chain Collars:** Some people, especially those with long-haired dogs, recommend chain collars, claiming that regular collars break the hair of long-haired dogs. Whether a dog should wear a chain collar must be decided by the owner, possibly with an experienced dog trainer. More important than the material is the protection against choking (slip stop) and good quality.

e) **Greyhound Collars:** These special collars are usually very wide, which makes sense given the long necks of many greyhounds. They often taper towards the buckle, so it is not too large. Greyhounds are usually doubly secured, meaning they are led with two collars. Due to their narrow head in contrast to their slightly broader neck, there is always the risk that the collar could slip over the ears, leaving the dog suddenly "collarless."

f) **Choke Collars/Endless Choke Chains and Prong Collars:** These are considered animal cruelty and are therefore banned in Germany. A brief description of these collars can be found at the end of this chapter.

3.2 Harness

The selection of harnesses is even more varied than that of collars. Depending on the original intended use, there are chest harnesses, tracking harnesses, saddle harnesses, pulling harnesses, training harnesses, guide harnesses, and more.

a) Chest Harnesses consist of a strap around the neck and one around the chest, connected by two straps (one at the top of the neck and one between the front legs). These harnesses often have three rings for the leash and are adjustable at the neck, chest, and sometimes between the front legs and rarely at the back.

b) Saddle Harnesses, like the so-called "Norwegian" harnesses, consist of a strap in front of the chest, held in place by a strap around the belly. The upper strap has a kind of "saddle" attached, to which bags, a lamp, or patches with funny slogans can be attached. Many assistance dogs wear saddle harnesses, which can be used as support harnesses with an additional handle. A support harness provides a person with balance issues or difficulty standing with support. Of course, the dog must be sufficiently large, absolutely healthy, and well-trained for this task!

c) Safety Harnesses have an additional strap behind the ribs, in addition to the straps around the neck and chest. They are largely "escape-proof."

d) Guide Harnesses are used in the context of assistance dogs. Depending on the person's disability, there are harnesses for blind, visually impaired, hearing impaired or deaf people, people with balance problems or gait uncertainties, autistic individuals, etc. Guide harnesses for assistance dogs always have a designation such as "Assistance Dog" or "Assistance Dog in Training" and rarely something similar. They are equipped with a long handle or an additional sturdy grip, allowing the handler to lean on it if needed or be guided.

Identification Vests are not harnesses! An identification vest is a special marker for assistance dogs and will be described later.

3.3 Leash

The leash is probably the oldest tool in human-dog coexistence. Humans likely used ropes early on to keep dogs in a certain place. These leashes were probably simply tied around the dog's neck. This basic form of a leash still exists today as the so-called "Moxon leash" or retriever leash. Leashes come in various materials, lengths, and designs, just like collars and harnesses.

Lead Leashes

Lead leashes are usually made of leather or webbing, solid-colored, multicolored, braided, or twisted. They always have at least one clasp to attach to a collar or harness. Lengths range from thirty centimeters (so-called short leads) to three meters. The longer leashes of usually two or three meters often have various rings and two clasps, allowing them to be adjusted to different lengths. For use with a Halti or head collar, there are now also leashes with two clasps of different weights: a lighter one for the Halti or head collar and a heavier one for the collar or harness.

Leather leashes are a bit more expensive but, with good care, can last a dog's lifetime. Webbing leashes can often be washed in the machine, and the new rubberized leashes or Biothane leashes can usually be wiped clean.

For all leashes, it is important: The clasp must match the leash and the dog's size! A clasp that is too light and of poor quality can break under heavy pull. A clasp that is too large and heavy constantly pulls on the collar or harness (gravity at work). The rule of thumb is: as large as necessary but as small and light as possible, and so that it can be easily handled by the person.

Other lead leashes include: Double Leashes: A leash with two clasps, e.g., for greyhounds or in combination with a safety harness. Coupler Leashes: For two, three, or even more dogs: a handle splits into several short leashes, each with a clasp.

Moxon Leash / Retriever Leash

Moxon leashes and retriever leashes have the same basic structure: A loop that serves as a collar transitions into a leash and a handle without any clasps or buckles. The big difference: Retriever leashes have two stops. These two stops prevent the collar part from unintentionally opening but, more importantly, from tightening endlessly. Thus, with correct adjustment, choking the dog is prevented. Classic Moxon leashes have no inward stop and can tighten to the point of choking. They are not allowed in Germany.

Moxon or retriever leashes also come in a variety of materials and colors. It is important to ensure that there are TWO stops to prevent the risk of choking. Moxon leashes WITHOUT two stops are considered cruel and are therefore prohibited. A brief description of these leashes can be found at the end of this chapter.

Long Leash

Long leashes are a very specific tool. They are essentially a three to twenty-meter long leash with a sturdy clasp attached to the DOG'S HARNESS. A long leash should never be attached to a collar! The risk of injury if the dog runs into the long leash with force is disproportionately high. Long leashes are often used in training to give the dog more freedom while still maintaining control. The classic use is recall training.

With the dog's increased movement radius, training can also occur over longer distances.

When using a long leash, gloves are highly recommended. A dog running at full speed on a ten-meter long leash gains considerable momentum over a radius of about twenty-two meters (ten meters from one end of the long leash to the other and the handler's arm length in between). Injuries, especially from the friction of the leash in the hand, are possible.

Handling the long leash must be practiced to avoid accidents for both humans and dogs. An experienced trainer should be consulted when getting used to and during the initial uses of the long leash.

Some dogs spend their entire lives on a long leash to give them at least a few meters of freedom, even if they do not reliably respond to recall. Subtypes of the long leash include trail leashes and tracking leashes.

Flexi Leash / Automatic Retractable Leashes

Flexi leashes, or automatic retractable leashes, divide the dog owner community into two very opposing camps. Some find them great and indispensable, while others completely reject them and seem to outright hate them. The fact is: A Flexi leash / automatic retractable leash is a long leash, usually three, five, or eight meters long, where the very thin leash is hidden in a small plastic housing. Unlike a long leash, the Flexi leash / automatic retractable leash only releases as much leash as the dog is currently away. Good Flexi leashes / automatic retractable leashes have a brake that can also be locked. The advantage of Flexi leashes / automatic retractable leashes is their relatively easy handling and the minimal dirt they collect.

The downside: The leashes are very thin and barely visible. Serious injuries can occur if an uninvolved person or dog runs into the leash or gets entangled in it.

Flexi leashes / automatic retractable leashes are also impractical for insecure dogs, as they can quickly slip out of hand. Very strong dogs can gain significant momentum with a Flexi leash and can cause their handler to fall.

One of the biggest arguments from dog trainers who oppose Flexi leashes / automatic retractable leashes: The dog learns to pull. As the leash automatically unwinds when the dog pulls, the dog quickly learns that pulling on the leash increases its radius. Recently, a manufacturer has offered three-meter retractable leashes in a small round housing that can be strapped around the wrist or to a wheelchair or walker. These very small leashes offer light or well-trained dogs a "free space" of about three meters.

3.4 Dummy / Treat Bag

The primary purpose of a dummy is to serve as a substitute for game during retrieval training. Dummies come in various designs, sizes, and colors. The classic dummies used in training are different-sized and weighted "fabric sausages," usually with a handle for easy grip. These dummies are placed or thrown, and the dog retrieves them on command. Treat dummies are small, typically round fabric bags that can be filled with treats. These should have both a zipper and a Velcro flap to prevent the dog from accessing the reward independently.

Since it is unnatural for a dog to relinquish its "prey," proper dummy work must be taught. The key is that the handler rewards the dog, not the dog opening the treat dummy itself. The dog should not play uncontrollably with the dummy or treat the dummy. These tools are training aids designed to enhance cooperation between the handler and the dog.

3.5 Additional Tools

3.5.1 Clicker

In the context of the three-second rule (see page 26), the clicker has become a popular tool in dog training. With practice and proper timing, the clicker is an excellent aid to reward the dog within the necessary three seconds. The "click" is not the reward but the promise of a reward. It confirms to the dog that its action is correct and that a reward is forthcoming.

Clicker training seems simple at first glance: a clicker, a few treats, and "click." However, it requires the dog to understand that "this strange noise means food." The clicker must be properly conditioned. Initially, every click, even a mis-timed one, results in a reward. Learning how to condition and use the clicker can be done through many dog training schools and workshops, as well as books and videos. Having an experienced trainer oversee the correct timing is highly beneficial for beginners.

Basic Clicker Conditioning:

The handler holds about ten small treats in one hand and the clicker in the other. With the dog attentive, the handler clicks once and IMMEDI-ATELY, preferably simultaneously, gives a treat to the dog. This is repeated until all the treats are used up.

In the second step, the handler waits until the dog is looking away but not highly distracted. A click sounds, and when the dog turns around, the reward is given. If the dog has understood the first step correctly, it should shift its gaze to the handler within seconds after the click.

In the third step, the handler checks if the dog has correctly understood the connection "click = treat." The handler waits until the dog is slightly distracted nearby. A click sounds, and the dog should immediately turn to the handler, looking for the treat.

CAUTION: Every click means a reward, even for a "mis-click." The handler must be very careful about which behavior they want to reward. Incorrect timing can lead to the dog learning unwanted behaviors. To prevent weight gain from treats during clicker training, the treats should be deducted from the daily food portion and kept as small as possible.

3.5.2 Target Stick

A target stick helps the dog learn to touch something with its nose or paw from a distance or maneuver to a specific position. Often used with a clicker, target sticks can be telescopically extended, making them compact when not in use but able to extend up to sixty centimeters during training. Most have a small colored ball at one end, making it easier for the dog to touch.

Training for "Nose Touch": Decide whether the dog will touch the target stick with its nose or paw. Using the nose is effective for most tasks.

Carefully ensure the dog touches the stick only with its nose, not with its tongue or teeth.Regularly check the target stick, especially the small ball, for damage and replace it if necessary.

3.5.3 Head Halter / Gentle Leader

A head halter, or Halti, allows better control of the dog, especially if the handler is smaller or weaker. Assistance dog trainees often go through phases of pulling on the leash or being very distracted. The head halter, placed around the dog's head like a horse halter, lets the handler direct the dog's gaze and attention.

Acclimating the Dog to the Head Halter: Gently accustom the dog to wearing the head halter with patience and guidance from an experienced trainer.

Practice handling two leashes: one attached to the collar or harness, and a second lighter leash attached to the head halter. The second leash is used to guide the dog's head and should remain slack unless needed.

A head halter should always be a temporary solution. Assistance dogs should not pull or be easily distracted unless it is part of their task.

3.5.4 Dog Backpack or Carrying Bags

There is a difference between a dog backpack, which the dog wears, and a carrying bag, which the dog carries in its mouth. Saddlebags attached to a harness allow the dog to carry provisions, first aid supplies, or lighter purchases on hikes. Trainers use saddlebags to give the dog a task and engage it better. Fitting and training with saddlebags require guidance from an experienced trainer.

Carrying bags, held in the dog's mouth, are suitable for light items but prevent the dog from performing tasks requiring its nose or mouth.

3.5.5 Identification Vest

The identification vest is the most noticeable tool of assistance dogs. Resembling a small dog coat, it always has the inscription "Assistance Dog" or "Assistance Dog in Training," sometimes specifying the dog's role (e.g., Alert Dog, Guide Dog).

In Germany, legal requirements for identification vests currently apply only to guide dogs for the blind. Most vests are red, yellow, or blue, while white vests or guide harnesses are reserved exclusively for guide dogs for the blind.

3.5.6 Wheelchair Leash

A wheelchair leash is designed to attach to a wheelchair, preventing accidental twisting with two swivel connectors. Typically about one meter long, it allows the dog to walk comfortably beside the wheelchair and perform assistance tasks. If the handler has limited hand motor skills, a retriever leash can simplify attaching the leash.

3.5.7 Autism Leash and Autism Harness

For some assistance tasks, it is necessary for the handler and the assistance dog to be connected by a leash. This is particularly common for individuals with Autism Spectrum Disorder (ASD) or Fetal Alcohol Syndrome (FAS). A connection via an autism leash can also be beneficial for people with a lack of danger awareness or limited cognitive abilities.

It is important that the autism leash is attached to a well-fitting dog harness and is comfortable for the handler to wear. There are special autism harnesses designed for children. For older handlers, an individual attachment solution often needs to be found. The leash should be only long enough for the dog to keep the child safe from dangers such as the street. Often, the dog is guided by another (adult) person who directs both the handler and the dog. If the leash is too long, the handler can still get into dangerous situations, such as stepping into the street, even if the dog is standing or walking with the caregiver. A length of about fifty centimeters has proven to be effective.

In German-speaking countries, the use of autism leashes is sometimes passionately debated. In other countries, this specialized tool is standard. Ultimately, each handler must decide together with their training facility.

3.6 Behavior Interrupters

Behavior interrupters are highly controversial in dog training. These "tools" are meant to interrupt and stop a dog from engaging in undesirable behavior. They should never be used as punishment, as the dog would not understand this. The most common behavior interrupters are throw chains, bells, rattling cans, water bottles, and spray collars.

Throw chains are small metal chains that produce a more or less loud clattering sound when shaken. Dogs are still taught to fear this metallic clatter by associating it with an unpleasant experience during conditioning.

The same principle applies to bells. Several metal plates connected by a string produce a metallic noise, which is initially linked to an unpleasant experience in training.

Rattling cans or clattering cans also work on this principle: the noise is associated with an unpleasant experience. Often, these behavior interrupters are a (usually metal) can filled with stones, metal pieces, coins, or similar, then tightly sealed.

A water bottle is used to squirt a jet of water at the dog when it displays unwanted behavior.

A spray collar is a tight-fitting collar with a small plastic box containing a battery, a spray nozzle, and, depending on the type, a scent or compressed air. With a remote control held by the handler, the spray mechanism can be activated from a distance. Usually, there are different intensity levels, ranging from a warning tone to a light spray to a more intense spray.

None of these tools have any place in assistance dog training. If a behavior interruption is necessary, it can be achieved with a carefully selected assistance dog using the interrupt command.

If the interrupt command is truly ineffective, an experienced assistance dog trainer can help.

3.7 Animal Welfare Violation "Tools"

As previously mentioned, some tools are still considered violations of animal welfare laws in Germany and many other European countries. Their use is sometimes prohibited and sometimes not clearly regulated. These so-called tools have no place in assistance dog training!

a) Choke Chains: Choke chains, which tighten completely when pulled, can cause the dog severe pain and even breathing difficulties. Therefore, these choke chains (without a stop mechanism) are prohibited by animal welfare laws.

b) Prong Collars: These are made of metal and have "prongs" or metal hooks on one side. Prong collars are also available with a leather cover, concealing the prongs. Regardless of whether the prongs are visible or hidden, prong collars are considered highly problematic from an animal welfare perspective because they cause the dog pain with every pull. In some countries, prong collars are legally banned.

c) Slip Leads WITHOUT Two Stoppers: These consist of a continuous piece of material. The issue is that without an "inner" stopper, the lead can tighten indefinitely, cutting into the dog's neck and restricting its breathing. Slip leads with an inner stopper are allowed but carry the risk of uncontrolled opening, releasing the dog.

d) Training Harnesses: There are various types of training harnesses, most of which create an unpleasant sensation when the dog pulls. Some "whistle" at a high pitch, while others constrict the front legs just below the elbows. The use of training harnesses must be very well considered, and they must fit 100% accurately, ideally used only under the supervision of an experienced trainer.

Two "tools" that have no place in assistance dog training: an electric shock collar (right) and a prong collar (left).

Afterword

These are the basic commands for assistance tasks. Any team that masters these basic commands has a solid foundation for a smooth and trusting partnership. These basic commands are also included in most assistance dog exams, and many public institutions and airlines require them. However, this list is not exhaustive, and in countries with regulated assistance dog exams, additional commands are often required. Consulting with the examiner or the examining institution can help avoid misunderstandings and surprises. If you have questions or difficulties in training, a session with an experienced assistance dog trainer can often help. Sometimes it is beneficial to take a step back in training and take a short break.

I greatly enjoyed compiling these basics. A big THANK YOU goes to my friends Tanja and Martin for their input on clarity, to Torsten W., without whose motivation this work would probably still be in the drawer, and to Kerstin G., who continually motivates and supports me.

I wish you and your four-legged partner a wonderful time together and all the best.

Sincerely, Katharina Küsters

Notice

Source of images

Patricia Stroucken, Meckenheim / Germany: Site 32, 77, 88, 89, 95, 113, 120, 123, 130

Site 6: AnnaGoroshnikova/Shutterstock

Site 10: MPH Photos/Shutterstock

Site 13: Duncan Andison /Shutterstock

Site 15: cynoclub/Shutterstock

Site 20: /Shutterstock

Site 27: Juninat/Shutterstock

Site 29: David Pegzlz/Shutterstock

Site 37: privat

Site 40: NewAfrika /Shutterstock

Site 43: GoodFocused/Shutterstock

Site 45: Suchada Taechotirote/Shutterstock

Site 47: anjajuli/Shutterstock

Site 50:Tibanna79 /Shutterstock

Site 52: GoodFocused/Shutterstock

Site 62: Anna Goroshnikova/Shutterstock

Site 67: SpeedKingz/Shutterstock

Site 70: IKO-studio/Shutterstock

Site 73: Blazej Lyjak/Shutterstock

Site 82: Micimakin/Shutterstock

Site 87: Jus_Ol/Shutterstock

Site 91: NewAfrika /Shutterstock

Site 96: Javier Brosch/Shutterstock

Site 101: Shutterstock

Site 103: SasaStock/Shutterstock

Site 108: Nalaphotos/Shutterstock

Site 112: Natalia Fedosova/Shutterstock

Site 117: Lisa Eastman/Shutterstock

Site 118: istanbulphotos/Shutterstock